71017

D0296683

71 0174143 7

LEEDS BECKETT UNIVERSITY

DISCARDED

LEEDS POLYTECHNIC - BECKETT PARK LIBRARY

The Public School Revolution

JOHN RAE

The Public School Revolution

BRITAIN'S INDEPENDENT SCHOOLS
1964–1979

FABER AND FABER
London & Boston

First published in 1981
by Faber and Faber Limited
3 Queen Square London WC1N 3AU
Printed in Great Britain by
Redwood Burn Limited, Trowbridge, Wiltshire
All rights reserved

© *John Rae, 1981*

710 174143-7

LEEDS POLYTECHNIC

367022 V

BPE

38424

373.25

19 JAN 1982   £6.50

British Library Cataloguing in Publication Data

Rae, John
The public school revolution.
1. Public schools, endowed (Great Britain)
I. Title
373.2′22′0941   LA634
ISBN 0-571-11789-9

To
the boys and girls
of
Westminster School
*with my gratitude
and respect*

Contents

Introduction

Britain's independent schools are a subject of controversy but even their most hostile critics would grant that the schools have an extraordinary capacity for survival. This capacity has never been more tested than in the fifteen years between 1964 and 1979. Inflation, political attack and social upheaval combined to challenge the schools' traditional attitudes and to threaten their future. How the schools responded is the theme of this book.

As the headmaster of an independent school during this period I am aware that I have been too close to the events to see them all in the correct perspective. As a historian I am aware that I also lack the perspective of time. On the other hand I have the advantage of personal knowledge of how and why changes were made and as Chairman of the Headmasters' Conference in 1977 I experienced at first hand the pressures that threaten the independent sector from without and the tensions and rivalries that threaten it from within. My account is a personal view, not a definitive history. I hope that at some time in the future, the history of the independent schools in these turbulent years will be written with greater detachment.

But the theme is too important to leave until then. The lessons of 1964–79 are needed today not only by the independent schools but also by their opponents. As I write this, the Labour Party is returning to the attack and schools are sending out to their parents the news that fees will have to rise by up to 35 per cent in the autumn. Survival is a continuing problem.

I have had access to a number of official records and to the opinions and recollections of people involved in the story. I have not wished, however, to burden the text with footnotes or a bibliography. A great many individuals responded to my appeal for information. There are too many to list individually but I am none the less very grateful to them for their help. I am particularly indebted to the following for reading parts of the manuscripts or for contributing especially valuable information: Lindsay Anderson, Sir Robert Birley, John Dancy, Tim Devlin, Frank Fisher, T. E. B. Howarth, Revd Alec Knight, Donald Lindsay, John Morris, Alan Mould, John Singleton. Any errors that remain are my responsibility alone.

Finally, I am very grateful to my family. It is bad enough to have a husband and father who is a headmaster; when he spends his holidays writing a book about schools it requires a special degree of tolerance and understanding on the part of his wife and children. For that tolerance and understanding, much thanks.

Westminster School
July 1980

I

The Challenges and the Schools

Between 1964, when Harold Wilson's Labour Government came into office, and 1979, when James Callaghan's fell, Britain's independent schools faced and overcame a formidable combination of challenges. For the first time in their long history they were confronted by a government that was not only hostile but explicitly committed to ending their independence. This political threat remained throughout the period; even during the four years of Conservative rule Labour spokesmen made it clear that when their party was returned to power the abolition of independent schools would be a priority. In September 1973, Roy Hattersley, the Party's Shadow Education Minister, put it bluntly to a conference of independent-school headmasters: 'I must, above all else, leave you with no doubts about our serious intention initially to reduce and eventually to abolish private education in this country.'

The political threat to the existence of independent schools coincided with what seemed to headmasters and headmistresses at the time a more immediate and perplexing challenge. The marked shift in educational opinion and the social upheaval in the late sixties, particularly in its effect on young people, challenged many of the schools' accepted attitudes and traditions. The fashionable rejection of competition, of streaming by ability and of academic selection challenged the independent schools to decide whether they would follow the fashion or, by resisting, place a much greater emphasis on academic excellence than most of them had done in the past. At the same time the fashionable rejection of authority challenged the schools to look critically at the structure of relationships that had for so long been regarded as an essential part of the public school experience.

In the wake of this educational and social challenge came yet another which, from the point of view of schools whose income depended on parents' ability to pay fees, was probably the most dangerous of all. The Public Schools Commission warned in 1968: 'If there were a lengthy economic recession in the country they [the public schools] might fail to weather the storm.' The recession occurred a few years later. The inflationary crisis of 1973–9, one of the most acute in British history, first doubled and then almost trebled the fees in independent schools. It was widely believed that the schools were rapidly pricing themselves out of the market and that as a result numbers must fall and schools must close. Abolitionists were persuaded that it was only a matter of time before economic pressure forced the schools out of business or into the arms of the maintained sector.

That the independent schools overcame all these challenges is not altogether surprising: they have shown remarkable resilience in the past. What was unexpected was that they should emerge from the testing time to all appearances stronger than they were before: the political threat had not been implemented; the fashions and unrest of the late sixties, far from weakening the schools, had enabled them to reform abuses and modernize the education they offered; and despite inflation there was no shortage of applicants. Perhaps even more important, the schools were more united than ever before and their morale and self-confidence were high.

It is this story of challenge and response, of changes, some of which in the context of the schools' history were revolutionary, that forms the subject of the present book. The subject has an importance beyond education. The history of British society in the last 500 years has been profoundly affected by the way in which its education system has developed. Unlike the great continental powers of France and Prussia which established early in the nineteenth century systems of national secondary education, the British relied on private enterprise. When at the end of the century parliament decided that government must take responsibility for secondary education, the independent schools were at the height of their prestige and influence. The young state—or, as it is correctly called, maintained—sector, had to grow up in the shadow of independent schools that not only enjoyed unchallenged supremacy but were patronized by the most powerful and influential groups in society—the upper class, the professional class and the wealthy businessmen. In no other country did independent schools hold this dominant position. That the schools should have retained this position so long through two world wars, the loss of empire and the rise of the welfare state, is open to different interpretations. Some see it as evidence of British respect for excellence and independence: to others it is proof that the British are wedded to obsolete attitudes of class and privilege. Few would agree with the critic who declared that the independent schools were irrelevant to the country's future. The schools' ability to emerge with renewed strength from the challenges of the sixties and seventies under-lines not only their resilience but also the fact that they cannot be ignored. For good or ill, the independent schools remain a potent factor in British society.

Anyone who sets out to write about independent schools in Britain faces the problem of definition. What schools is he talking about? It seems a simple enough question but in British education, particularly in its independent sector, nothing is as simple as it seems. Until recently the term 'independent schools' was seldom used. People spoke of maintained or state schools on one hand and of public schools on the other, to the confusion of foreigners who could not understand in what sense private schools could be public.

That the term 'public school' should be obsolescent is something of a triumph for the schools' public relations. In the early seventies the heads of independent schools were anxious to bury the term 'public school' as quickly and decently as possible. This was partly because, in the face of political threats, the old-established public schools decided to throw in their lot with all recognized independent schools. A more important, if less publicly acknowledged, reason for a change of nomenclature was

the desire of the heads to dissociate themselves and their schools
from the overtones of snobbery and exclusiveness that to the
British ear were immediately audible in the words 'public
school'.

They were so successful that even the Labour Party, which had
everything to gain from sticking to the old loaded terminology,
nevertheless dropped it altogether for their 1979 manifesto. The
'public schools', which had for so long provoked extremes of
loyalty and revulsion, became the 'independent schools', a title
that was not only more accurate but which suggested—as it was
intended to do—liberty and individual enterprise. Few British
people could be expected to rally to the defence of the public
schools, but independence was a wider and more fundamental
issue. The term 'public school' had implied privilege: the term
'independent school' seemed to raise a question of principle. If a
government crushed independence in education where might it
strike next?

There are over 2,000 independent schools in Britain. Of these
about 1,350 are recognized as efficient by the Department of
Education and Science. The remainder are known as 'registered
schools': they meet certain criteria of health and safety laid down
by the Department but they do not meet the educational criteria.
Of the 1,350 recognized independent schools, just over a
thousand are members of ISIS—the Independent Schools
Information Service—and recognize the leadership, in policy
matters, of the Independent Schools Joint Council (ISJC). It is
with these one thousand schools that this book is concerned.

The ISIS schools educate some 360,000 boys and girls between
the ages of five and eighteen. This total represents a very small
percentage of all the school children in this age group. The
numbers in all independent schools (not just the ISIS schools)
represents 3·5 per cent of the five-to-eleven age group and 5·3
per cent of the twelve-and-over age group. Taking all age groups,
including the nursery stage, the percentage of children in
independent schools in Britain is 4·4.

These percentages can be misleading however and have
persuaded some commentators that the independent sector is too

small to affect British education one way or the other. But the higher the age group, the larger the percentage in independent schools, because while these schools are not strong at the nursery level they offer what is arguably the best sixth-form education in the country. At the same time a much higher proportion of independent-school pupils stay on in the sixth form, partly, it is true, because their parents can afford to let them do so, but primarily because they have the ability to tackle an A-level course. Thus, 23 per cent of all pupils taking three or more A-levels are in independent schools. This point is often missed by politicians who are reluctant to acknowledge that independent schools are educating a significant part of any age group. When the Labour Government launched its Great Debate on education in 1977 it did not invite independent schools to take part even though they were educating a quarter of the most able pupils in the country.

There are a number of distinct groups within the ISIS schools. The headmasters of the oldest, richest and most prestigious boys' secondary schools are members of the Headmasters' Conference, an organization started by Edward Thring of Uppingham in 1869 to discuss the public schools' response to the Endowed Schools Act, the first political threat to the schools' independence. I have used the term 'public schools' when I wish to refer to those boys' secondary schools whose headmasters are in membership of the Headmasters' Conference rather than to all independent schools; and I have used the term 'Great Schools' when I wish to refer to the handful of famous schools—Eton, Winchester, Westminster, Rugby and so on—that from the early nineteenth century have been uppermost in the minds of opponents and supporters alike when they have spoken of public schools. To identify an élite group in this way may seem to reinforce that obsession with a school's precise standing in the hierarchy that has been (and to some degree still is) such an unattractive aspect of the independent-school world. I have no wish to do this but I need a convenient shorthand for this group of schools, not because they are better than others but because they are of such symbolic and pyschological importance.

There are 210 members of the Conference, including seventy-six heads of ex-direct grant schools that have chosen to go independent rather than join the maintained sector. The snobbish quibble as to whether they should all be called public schools, a characteristic English diversion for almost a century, is now forgotten except by a few parents who, having paid the price, wish it to be known that their sons are attending a real public school. There is a lingering tension, however, within the Conference between the so-called Great Schools and the less well-known, smaller and newer schools, but this tension has more to do with a suspicion that the heads of the Great Schools are calling the tune in the Conference than with envy of the Great Schools' pre-eminence in the public eye.

The Society of Headmasters of Independent Schools contributes thirty-five schools to the membership of ISIS. These are boys' secondary schools whose academic performance does not meet the criteria laid down for membership of the Headmasters' Conference. Since there are a number of schools in the Conference who no longer meet the academic criteria themselves, there is here, too, a possible source of tension within the independent sector.

The girls' schools' equivalent of the Headmasters' Conference is the Girls' Schools' Association, whose 204 secondary schools are all members of ISIS. At the primary or preparatory level, there are 442 boys' and 130 girls' schools belonging to ISIS through their membership of the Incorporated Association of Preparatory Schools (IAPS) and the Association of Headmistresses of Preparatory Schools (AHPS) respectively.

In addition to all these schools there is a group of about forty independent secondary schools which belong to none of these organizations yet who qualify for membership of ISIS through their membership of the boys' or girls' association of governing bodies. These include at least one school, Millfield, that has established itself as a leading independent school despite the continued reluctance of the Headmasters' Conference to elect it to membership.

The opponents of independent schools seldom concern them-

18

selves with these nice distinctions between different groups; all independent schools are swept up in the general condemnation. Yet it is the boys' public schools, the commanding heights of the independent sector, that have always provoked and that still provoke the strongest hostility.

2

Critical Themes Before 1964

The independent schools have seldom lacked critics. The nature of criticism may have changed over the centuries but there are recurring themes, and the contemporary case for the abolition of these schools cannot be fully understood outside the historical context. I propose therefore in this chapter to look at the criticisms of the past and to see how far, if at all, the criticisms led to effective action.

The history of Britain's independent public schools begins in 1382 with William of Wykeham's foundation of Winchester College. Winchester was the first public school, public in the sense that its entry was neither local nor restricted but open to 'poor scholars' and to the 'sons of noble and influential persons' drawn from different parts of the country. Public also in the sense of being in contrast to the private tutor favoured by many aristocratic families for the education of their sons. Other schools have, with considerable ingenuity and occasional dishonesty, claimed greater antiquity than Winchester but they miss the point. There were schools in England before 1382 and some of their descendants still exist but they were not public schools in the sense I have described. It is the foundation of Winchester that marks the start of that peculiarly English phenomenon, the public school.

Winchester's foundation was followed by that of Eton in 1440 and these two schools, together with Westminster (refounded in 1560 by Queen Elizabeth after the second dissolution of the Benedictine monastery), held a dominant position among the public schools until the second half of the eighteenth century when Westminster declined and Winchester, trapped in medi-evalism, could offer little competition to Eton's now un-questioned pre-eminence. These three were known as the 'Great Schools' but there were others which, though not yet thought of as having the same special character, were nevertheless to form, with Eton, Winchester and Westminster, the core of the public school system as it developed in the nineteenth century. They were the charitable foundations such as Christ's Hospital and the Charterhouse, the great London day schools such as St. Paul's and the handful of grammar schools such as Harrow, Rugby and Shrewsbury, which developed a national and not merely a local reputation.

Long before the nineteenth century the principal critical themes had become clear. The most important and persistent criticism centred on the characteristically English concern with social class. In its earliest form the criticism argued that schools founded for the education of all classes, including poor scholars, had been taken over by the sons of the aristocracy. In its latest form it argues that the schools represent privilege and social division.

The evidence suggests that in their early period, that is to say between the fourteenth and the seventeenth centuries, the public schools did educate boys from different social classes, the son of the plumber and the basketmaker alongside the sons of gentle-men and aristocrats. The lines of social division were not as clearly drawn as they were to be in the eighteenth and nineteenth centuries. But the interaction between social class and educa-tional opportunity that has bedevilled the development of education in this country was very soon in evidence. In 1540 there was an exchange on this subject in relation to the Grammar School at Canterbury, between the Commissioners headed by Lord Rich who were considering the future of the school and the Archbishop, Thomas Cranmer. It is worth quoting because the arguments of the Commissioners illustrate so clearly a view of the nature and purpose of education that was to be reinforced over and over again by the attitude of the public schools.

The Commissioners argued that the sons of the poor should not be given what we should call an academic education because they were to become ploughmen and artificers. It was only the children of gentlemen who should be 'put to school'. To this Cranmer replied: 'Poor men's children are many times endued with more singular gifts of nature which are also gifts of God, as with eloquence, memory, apt pronounciation, sobriety, and such like, and also commonly more apt to apply their study than is the gentleman's son delicately nurtured.' But the Commissioners insisted that 'it was more meet for the ploughman's son to go to plough and the artificer's son to apply the trade of his parent's vocation, and the gentleman's children are meet to have the knowledge of government and rule in the commonwealth.' Cranmer did not agree; if the poor man's son was more apt he should be admitted to the school in preference to the son of a gentleman. Merit, not birth, should be the criterion for entry.

Cranmer's view, the view of all those subsequently who have believed in equality of opportunity, prevailed at Canterbury, but it was the Commissioners' view of opportunity dictated by class that increasingly prevailed in the public schools. The better the schools became, the more they were in demand and the harder it became for the ploughman's and artificer's son to gain entry. When Dr Busby in the seventeenth century made Westminster the first really successful school, at which it was a positive advantage to have been educated, the aristocracy abandoned the private tutor and sent their sons there.

The immediate effect was that the scholars on the foundations of the Great Schools were soon outnumbered by the Oppidans or Townboys. Where the scholars or free-place boys were drawn from a class that could not pay, it was common practice for them to be segregated from the fee-payers in case the latter were contaminated by the former: the free-place boys sat separately in class divided, in some schools, by a physical partition 'breast-high', and used the playground at different times. It was a way of meeting the criticism of men such as Dean Swift, who wrote in 1723 that 'the public schools, by mingling the sons of the nobleman with those of the vulgar, engage the former in bad company.'

A hundred years later Swift would have had no cause for anxiety. The sons of the vulgar had effectively been excluded from the old public schools, while many of the new schools founded in the first half of the nineteenth century explicitly restricted entry to the 'sons of gentlemen'. It was this development that fed the mounting radical criticism of the public schools. The critics blamed the schools, not only for betraying the wishes of their founders, but also for creating class distinctions. There were calls for government action to reform the schools.

To these criticisms the public schools responded with arguments that they have used ever since. They did not create class distinction, they merely reflected it. Given the hardening lines of class division in British society, it was inevitable that difficulties would arise if they tried to educate the gentleman's and the ploughman's sons together. 'It is not the fault of the boys,' the headmaster of Repton argued in the 1860s, 'it is the fault of society. I never saw a man yet who would send his boy to a school in order to associate with those lower than himself.'

When attacked on the question of privilege, the public schools appealed to a higher tribunal—the principle of independence. They argued—then as now—that government interference would be disastrous and contrary to the wishes of the founders, whose intentions had clearly been to establish independent schools. That they had become almost exclusively upper-class institutions did not seem to concern them at all. They were educating the sons of the most influential people in the country and they could afford to face their critics with confidence.

It is not surprising therefore that the two Commissions set up in the 1860s—the Clarendon and Taunton Commissions—did nothing to alter the class basis of the schools. On the contrary, some of their well-intentioned reforms had the opposite effect. They insisted that at the old schools, entry to the foundation, that is to say to a free or scholarship place, should be by competitive exam only. But, right though it obviously was in principle, it restricted the scholarships to those whose parents could afford the special tuition necessary to succeed in the examination. Some of the other recommendations of the Commissions explicitly reinforced the class basis of the schools' entry. At Harrow and Rugby, for example, the claims of the poor boys living in the neighbourhood were to be met by the establishment of separate schools, the logical extension of the breast-high partition. The schools were to be known by the names of the founders of the original schools, John Lyon at Harrow and Lawrence Sherriff at Rugby, and were to provide instruction 'such as may be suitable for boys intended for commercial and other similar occupations'. This was the next step in the argument put forward by Lord Rich in 1540: that the sons of the lower classes should go into occupations suitable for them while the sons of gentlemen are separately educated in the 'the knowledge of government and rule in the commonwealth'.

The period between the Clarendon and Taunton Commissions and the First World War was the golden age of the public school. The critics of the class orientation had been seen off. The criticisms of the moral and intellectual limitations of the schools had been met, at least to the satisfaction of the schools and their clientele, by the reforms of Dr Arnold at Rugby in the first half of the century and by those of Thring of Uppingham and Sanderson of Oundle in the second. Liberal, intellectual criticism continued but it touched the schools hardly at all. The critics were dismissed as social inferiors or intellectuals, two groups for whose opinion public school men had an instinctive contempt. 'You'll find plenty of fellows abusing Harrow,' says the hero's uncle in H. A. Vachell's novel *The Hill*, published in 1905, 'but take it from me the fault lies not in Harrow but in them. Such boys, as a rule, do not come out of the top drawer.' George Bernard Shaw might demand that 'Eton, Harrow, Winchester and their cheaper and more pernicious imitators should be razed to the ground and their foundations sown with salt', but there was not the slightest chance that anyone in power would listen, let alone act on his suggestion.

The schools themselves seem to have been unaware that their exclusiveness might be harmful to society. It is a point that public school headmasters found (and to some extent still do find) difficult to grasp. The schools were so much a reflection and a reinforcement of the class structure that they could hardly be expected to see that structure as something that was in itself wrong. When the schools were accused of widening class divisions, headmasters replied—then as now—with arguments about current affairs lectures and visits to the school's boys' club in the East End. In 1912, for example, when John Galsworthy accused the public schools of encouraging 'instincts of caste that forbid sympathy and understanding between the well-to-do and the poorer classes', Lionel Ford, the headmaster of Galsworthy's old school, Harrow, argued that this was not the case because he arranged lectures and missions to help his boys to develop a sense of 'brotherhood with the unfortunate'. But the lectures and missions, however well intentioned, were an integral part of the *status quo*. What public school headmasters seldom seem to have asked themselves was whether the *status quo* needed to be changed.

It is only in recent years that public school headmasters have expressed any regret at the lack of contact between their schools and the schools in the maintained sector. Isolation from the maintained schools in the first half of this century does not appear to have worried them at all. On the contrary they allowed their isolation to increase with the development of a network of privately owned preparatory schools whose sole purpose was to provide the entry to public schools at the age of thirteen. Since the transfer to secondary school in the maintained sector was at the age of eleven, this effectively precluded the use of maintained primary schools by the children who were intended for public school at the next stage. There were exceptional public schools that recruited at eleven, but they were not the fashionable or prestigious ones. By the 1920s it was common practice for the son of a wealthy family to be educated exclusively in private schools from the age of seven to eighteen, and then to go on to an almost equally class-based university at Oxford or Cambridge, so that at no point did he run the risk of meeting his contemporaries from other classes. 'Nowhere, in fact, is a deeper gulf to be found between the independent Public Schools and the general system of education,' reflected the Report of the Public Schools

Committee in 1944, 'than in the difference between the methods adopted to prepare boys to enter the two kinds of school.'

In the decade after the end of the First World War the criticisms of the public schools gathered momentum, particularly in the form of novels, but it was also a period of unprecedented demand for places at the schools, a factor that did not encourage a constructive response to the critics. The falling birth rate and the threat of economic disaster for the rich between 1928 and 1938 undermined confidence and created a crisis of empty places but without prompting change. During the Second World War there were increasing fears that in the post-war world the schools would be educational and social anachronisms. It was in this context that in 1942, R. A. Butler, the President of the Board of Education, asked Lord Fleming to head a committee to consider how the public schools could be brought into closer association with the general education system of the country. It was to be the last chance for the public schools to break out of their narrow class base. The Committee certainly took the point and when it reported in 1944, recommended that the schools should be opened, as Cranmer had wished, to all who would benefit by the education 'irrespective of the income of parents'. The schemes which the Committee proposed would, it confidently hoped, enable the schools 'to remedy the most serious weakness in the education they offer, derived from the fact that at present they too often concern themselves with children coming from only a limited section of society'.

But the hope was not fulfilled. Neither the Local Education Authorities nor the schools themselves showed much inclination to put the schemes into practice. When the Labour Party's Public Schools Commission reported in 1966, it looked back to 1944 and wrote 'It is clear that as an instrument of national policy the Fleming Report rapidly became a dead letter.'

Whether—as is sometimes claimed—a great opportunity was missed in 1944 is open to question; the public schools accepted the Report but in the post-war years of austerity few Local Education Authorities had the money to take up places even when the places were offered.

Sir Robert Birley was a member of the Fleming Committee. His assessment of why the recommendations of the Fleming Report were not implemented does not suggest that it was the public schools which were at fault:

> The crux of the question is to be found in the recommendation in the Report that the system of assisted places at the public schools should be administered and paid for by the Ministry of Education and the Treasury, although Local Education Authorities were to be allowed to have their own schemes if they wished. We discussed this question for hours. Our first idea was to put it in the hands of LEAs with some kind of regional grouping. But all our sympathetic LEA witnesses (and most were sympathetic) and the LEA representatives on the Committee itself said that this would be fatal. This was well expressed by one of the leading Directors of Education at the time who said to me, 'Do remember this. Men pay their taxes in sorrow but their rates in anger.' The amount spent on sending one boy to a fee-paying school would be at once noticeable to rate-payers, but not to tax-payers. . . .
>
> I think that if a Conservative Government had won the General Election of 1945, something on the lines of the Fleming Scheme would have been started. If so, I think that by now it would be regarded as quite commonplace. I think the Scheme would not have destroyed the independence of the public schools. However, Labour won the Election of 1945. They were not opposed to the Scheme in principle, I know (at least most of them were not). But they were not prepared to have a scheme run under the Ministry and the Treasury: the whole thing was to be run by LEAs. As soon as I heard of this decision, I realized the scheme was doomed. . . .
>
> I think I know the reason. When Labour came to power in 1945 there were few of them with much experience of *national* politics. But a very great many had had experience of *local* politics and many had served on Borough or County Councils with Labour majorities. They were extremely suspicious of anything which might seem to weaken the authority of local government. This became very clear in the debate over direct grant schools. Most Labour members then wanted to get hold of them. They felt them to be a kind of standing criticism of

local authorities. The Government did not abolish the direct grant status and the reason was that they decided not to risk a row with the Roman Catholic church. Ellen Wilkinson had to beat off an attack from her own party in the Commons and came back to the Ministry furious: 'There was I, having to support Roman Catholic schools—I, who don't believe in anything.'

Robert Birley was then headmaster of Charterhouse. In 1949 he became headmaster of Eton. During the 1950s he continued to press for the introduction of a scheme on the Fleming lines but with the criteria for admission to the public schools more clearly defined in term of need. But the political climate, which had been sympathetic to the idea in 1945, had now turned sour. Neither the Labour nor the Conservative Party was interested.

By the beginning of the period with which this book is concerned, the public schools were as much schools for the wealthy and influential as they had ever been. Graham Kalton's survey conducted in 1964–5 found that 84 per cent of public school boys had fathers in the Registrar General's social classes I and II, when in the male population as a whole these classes accounted for only 19 per cent. The figure for the boarding public schools was 92 per cent. Despite the critics and the commissions, despite the attempts by the schools themselves to open their doors wider, attempts that were sometimes genuine, sometimes disingenuous or half-hearted, the class basis of the public school system remained. The fact that there were some public schools, notably the direct grant schools, whose intake was much less socially exclusive, did little to mitigate criticism of the schools' social divisiveness.

Closely associated with the critique of their narrow social intake was the allegation that the schools formed part of a cycle of privilege whereby those in influential, élite positions in society ensured that their sons would also enjoy the advantages of high status occupations. It was, perhaps, an English version of the seventeenth-century French tax, the Paulette, that enabled French officials to pass their positions on to their sons for the payment of an annual sum to the government. So by paying an annual fee to the public school the English upper classes guaranteed a secure and socially prestigious career for their children. The public school headmasters might argue that their schools did not create social divisions but they could not deny that they reinforced them. Without the stamp of a well-known public school it required exceptional ability to enable a young man to break into the charmed circle of politics or the professions. With such a stamp, limited ability was no bar to preferment.

Criticism of the cycle of privilege, of the old-boy network, was slow to develop. The English seem to have accepted with remarkable equanimity the blend of nepotism and privilege that held the class structure in place. That a small group of public schools provided half the undergraduates at Oxford and Cambridge until well into the nineteenth century and that a few schools and colleges—Eton and King's, Winchester and New College, Westminster and Christ Church—were so closely linked by their foundations that the college was an undergraduate extension of the school, does not appear to have been regarded as anything other than the natural order of things.

From Oxford and Cambridge, the public school men moved on to dominate the Church, the Law, the Civil Service and the Universities. Others went directly from school to the Royal Military Academy at Sandhurst. The purchase of commissions in the army had been ended in 1871, but unless your parents had purchased a public school education your chances of being a commissioned officer—except in wartime—remained slight until the second half of this century. As late as the 1950s, two-thirds of the successful applicants to Sandhurst were public school boys. The chances of reaching senior rank were even smaller: a study in 1939 of Lieutenant Generals and above showed that 82 per cent came from public schools. In the navy and the air force, where command required specialized, technical competence, the preponderance of public school boys was not nearly so marked.

When criticism of the old-boy network began to be voiced—and this was not on a significant scale until after the Second World War—the defenders of the public schools argued that it was one of the particular properties of a public school education to inculcate qualities of leadership and that this, not unfair advantage or favouritism, accounted for the high proportion of public school men in senior positions. To which the critics replied that British leadership, whether in the public service or in private enterprise, had been singularly inept when compared with the leadership in our competitor countries which had not enjoyed the benefits of a public school system. In other words, the public schools not only provided a disproportionate number of leaders in British society but also ensured that those leaders were incompetent.

This was a further fundamental criticism of the public schools. They not only restricted their intake to a narrow social class. They not only reinforced privilege and inequality of opportunity. Their concept of leadership excluded those very qualities— imagination, vision, a willingness to innovate and an awareness of the importance of technological change—that were needed to make leadership effective. The public schools, the critics argued, produced loyal, reliable conformists, admirable men to police a far-flung empire but not for holding key positions in a century of rapid change. Historians now ask the question that was implicit in the criticisms of the past: can it be chance that Britain's long decline from the last quarter of the nineteenth century coincided exactly with that period in her history when the public schools and public school men were at the height of their influence? They point not only to the conformity required for survival in the late Victorian boarding school but also to the narrowness of the curriculum, in which the study of the classics predominated and science was a poor, even absent relation.

Finally, there were all those criticisms of the schools' lifestyle, criticisms that were in many ways less fundamental, but that nevertheless attracted the most public attention: that the schools were brutal, philistine societies, condoning homosexuality, in-stitutionalized sadism and the worship of games. These criticisms have a long history. Only the most fanatical supporter would deny that at some periods the schools deserved the criticisms. The question is how far the criticisms were still valid in the early 1960s. The schools claimed that they had changed and that such criticisms were out of date; their opponents argued that the changes were of degree and not of substance. The Headmasters' Conference was at this time sufficiently worried by the unfavourable image created by these criticisms to draw up a 'Programme for Action' which listed ten 'popular myths that need to be scotched'. These myths were that public schools:

(a) are a refuge for the brainless and the philistine
(b) are consecrated to Latin and teach no science
(c) are uninterested in sending boys to the new universities and Redbrick
(d) have privileged access to Oxbridge places, for example through closed awards
(e) monopolize the City, Sandhurst, Whitehall and the Bar
(f) do not send boys into industry and are disdainful of modern technology
(g) foster bullying and sadism, particularly through corporal punishment and fagging
(h) have barbaric living conditions
(i) enjoy an unfairly high staff-pupil ratio
(j) promote homosexuality.

Nothing more clearly indicates that all these criticisms were very much alive in the early 1960s than the determination of the Headmasters' Conference in this period to take the business of its public relations more seriously.

Over the centuries, criticism of the public schools has tended to rise and fall in intensity as a result of social and political factors that have had little to do with the schools themselves. The attacks on the public schools led by Lord Brougham in the period 1816–20 reflected the demand for political power by the new class that owed its wealth to the industrial revolution. A hundred years later the First World War provoked a new round of attacks but during the fifteen years of national recovery after the end of the Second World War, the attacks were muted. It is only with the 1960s that the latest round of serious attacks on the public schools began.

The reason for this most recent intensification is not difficult to understand. The social revolution of Attlee's post-war government had left the 'privileged sector' of education untouched. Thirteen years of Conservative government had done nothing to reconcile the critics to the schools' continued existence. On the contrary, the long period of Conservative rule provoked increasing criticism of the establishment and of those institutions associated with it. To a society that saw itself breaking free at last from the conventions and taboos of imperial Britain, the public schools appeared to be a peculiarly offensive anachronism. The prospect of a Labour victory in the next general election whetted the appetite for root-and-branch reform. In the autumn of 1963 Derek Wigram, the Chairman of the Headmasters' Conference, told his colleagues, 'It is not of our choosing that the public schools are the centre of acute controversy today.' But the critics disagreed: the public schools were the centre of controversy because they represented all that was wrong with British society. 'The public school system', wrote John Morgan in a particularly vitriolic attack in the *New Statesman* in February 1964, 'is the greatest single source of the present British malaise which, as we all know, takes the form, Centaur-like, of amateurism at the top and a lack of opportunity below.'

Morgan's article reflected the anger and impatience of those who wanted the public schools to be done to death by an incoming Labour Government. Social change was in the air. The concept of social injustice was much discussed. The public schools' apparent inability to grasp this concept intensified the demands for their abolition. John Morgan argued: 'Public school boys seem to find it difficult to comprehend—I want to be cool and reasonable about this—the hysterical rage, the inarticulate fury, that the existence of independent fee-paying schools can inspire. . . . It is a rage against injustice.'

It was against this background of increasingly bitter criticisms of their schools that headmasters awaited with some anxiety the outcome of the 1964 election.

3

The Political Challenge 1964–1979

The Attitude of the Labour Party

Harold Wilson's 1964 Labour Government was the first to come into office with the clear intention of tackling the problem of the public schools. The Party's election manifesto was explicit: 'Labour will set up an educational trust to advise on the best way of integrating the public schools into the state system of education.'

Before 1964, the issue of the public schools had never been mentioned in a Labour election manifesto. By 1970, the issue had disappeared again, the manifesto of that year contenting itself with a vague statement that 'the education system must not perpetuate educational and social inequalities.' In 1974, the issue reappeared but only in the form of a pledge to withdraw 'all forms of tax relief and charitable status of public schools'. But the pledge was never fulfilled. Like the policy of integration, the withdrawal of charitable status was much talked about but never implemented. When it came to the point the Labour Party appeared to lack the will to destroy or even weaken the enemy it had stalked so long.

From its earliest days the Labour Movement regarded the public schools as one of its enemies. Like the House of Lords, the schools perpetuated the privilege and inequality that the Movement was determined to remove. Labour intellectuals hated the schools for their snobbery and philistinism; and also perhaps because so many Labour intellectuals had themselves been educated at public schools. Labour's rank and file, excluded from

33

the schools, were happy to destroy them. The degree of hostility to the schools is to be found in the resolutions to the Party's annual conference rather than in the election manifestoes. A 1970 resolution catches exactly that blend of radical politics and righteous indignation that characterizes Labour's antagonism to the schools over the last half-century. The public schools leave their opponents, if not exactly speechless with rage, then at least struggling in the cross-currents of reason and emotion. The 1970 resolution recommended 'a planned attack on the so-called public schools, this bastion of privilege and royal road to positions of power and influence, particularly in the upper reaches of the Civil Service. . . .'; and it called on the next Labour Government 'to take early action to end the private sector of education'.

But this passion has not been translated into action. In the first half of this century that failure was hardly surprising. The Labour Party was not in a position to initiate radical reform. Its manifestoes of the period speak of equality of opportunity in education but this had to remain an elusive ideal. In 1945, however, the sweeping Labour victory gave the party a chance to act. Certainly many of those who voted Labour must have believed that the end of the public schools was at hand. Yet Clement Attlee's 1945–51 Government never posed a threat to the schools. To attribute this—as some left-wingers do—to the fact that key members of the Cabinet, including the Prime Minister himself, had been educated at public schools is an attractive but unconvincing thesis. Harold Wilson's Cabinet had a higher proportion of former public school boys but it did not hesitate to initiate action against the schools. The truth is that Attlee's Government had more important things to do. It embarked on a major programme of domestic reform. In education its priority was to extend and improve the maintained system. The question of public schools was not forgotten. It was postponed.

For Attlee's Government, as for any Labour Government whose political flavour is social democratic, there was also a dilemma. How does a democracy set about abolishing independent institutions, particularly if those institutions are functioning efficiently and within the law? Those within the

Labour Movement who have called for the end of the public schools have never explained how such a policy is to be reconciled with the demands of liberty. It is this dilemma, more than any other factor, that has frustrated the desire of those who believe that the existence of a private sector of education is an affront to social justice.

While the Labour Party was in opposition between 1951 and 1964, the demands for the abolition of public schools intensified, so much so that Party headquarters thought it necessary to underline the dilemma that the Party faced. The Party's *Notes for Speakers*, issued in 1958, explained the dilemma and made a characteristically vague proposal as to how the dilemma could be resolved.

There are many viewpoints about the public schools within the Labour Movement. There are those who would like to see the public schools 'abolished'. But it is difficult to see how this could be done. Just as it was found impossible, in introducing the National Health Service, to forbid the existence of a private nursing home, so it is difficult in a democracy to forbid parents to pay for sending their children to independent schools if they choose to spend their money in this way.

Others believe that the public schools should be democratized, either by taking them over or by abolishing fees or by compelling them to offer 50 or 60 per cent of free places, as many independent schools do today. This solution is open to the serious objection that it accentuates the existing segregation of a scholarship élite.

There is a third school of thought, which believes that if enough comprehensive schools are built the public schools will die a natural death. This is an optimistic belief.

It would be a mistake to try to solve the public school problem in the next Party programme. It is obvious the nation cannot tolerate for ever the existence of a small number of fee-paying 'prep' schools and 'public' schools with smaller classes and a high social prestige alongside the state system. Such schools, especially if their number were allowed to expand, would draw the top stream from the comprehensive schools, thus helping to defeat the main object of the comprehensive school.

35

Eventually, local authorities may be able to work into their development plans provision for the utilization of the public schools as part and parcel of the general scheme. It will probably be thought best that such schools should be used exclusively for the benefit of the over-fifteens, who will best be able to retain that which is good in the existing system. But there must be a lot of progress before such steps can be undertaken on the road outlined by this programme.

The final paragraph is virtually meaningless and was probably intended to be so. Party headquarters knew there was no way out of the dilemma. But that knowledge only served to increase the frustration felt by many Labour activists. This frustration was already helping to switch Labour's attention away from the public schools and on to the selective grammar schools in the maintained system. If the Party could not eliminate the inequality represented by the public schools, it could remove what it regarded as inequality in the maintained system. In its 1955 manifesto, the Party pledged itself to 'a radical reform of our educational service'. This did not mean an attack on the public schools but upon the Eleven-Plus selection procedure which divided maintained-school children into those suitable for an academic education at grammar school and those for whom a less academic course at a secondary modern school was thought to be appropriate. Like Thomas Cranmer in the sixteenth century, the Labour Party rejected the idea that there should be two types of education based on class: an academic one for the sons of gentlemen and a practical one for the sons of ploughmen and artificers. The defenders of the grammar schools claimed that class had nothing to do with it and that children, regardless of their background, had different aptitudes which the education system should reflect.

The abolition of selection at Eleven-Plus in maintained schools was seen by the Labour Party (and by many outside it) as an important step towards a fairer, more homogeneous society. Selection not only denied opportunities to the less able, it also divided the community. By making the secondary schools comprehensive in their intake, the Labour Party believed it was being consistent with its aim, stated as long ago as 1924, of providing 'equality of opportunity in education'. It was also doing something to compensate for the frustration of being unable to abolish the public schools.

By 1955, the Party had firmly committed itself to the abolition of selection and to the absorbing of the grammar schools into a new comprehensive system. But not all Labour's leaders thought this policy was correct. Dick Crossman, one of Labour's most powerful intellectuals, argued that by abolishing the grammar schools with their long tradition of scholarship, the Party would give a new lease of life to the public schools which would snap up those parents who were disenchanted with comprehensive education. The experience of the last fifteen years suggests that, in the short run at least, Crossman was right.

Nor did the attack on the grammar schools enable Labour to escape from the fundamental dilemma posed by the public schools. On the contrary, the dilemma was made more acute. While there were grammar schools, the bright child from the poor home could obtain a good education free. But as the maintained system struggled with the difficult task of 'going comprehensive', academic standards appeared to fall. Simultaneously, the public schools, only a few of which had been as academic as the old grammar schools, turned their attention increasingly to academic affairs and selected their pupils on academic attainment rather than on family connection. In other words the public schools filled the academic vacuum left by the disappearance of the grammar schools.

When Labour saw what was happening, the public school issue became a live one again. These schools (including the direct grant schools) were accused of 'creaming off' the most able children and the most articulate parents. It was claimed that the comprehensive schools would never reach their true potential while this creaming off continued. It was for this reason that when Harold Wilson became leader of the Labour Party in 1963, he could not postpone the question of the public schools as so many of his predecessors had done.

In the 1964 election campaign, education was not an issue. If

37

the electors could be said to have voted for action on the public schools, it is only in the most general sense that they were voting for the whole package of Wilson's new deal. Wilson himself never showed much interest in the question but he was shrewd enough to recognize that this time the Party expected something to be done. Within a year of his election victory he had redeemed his election pledge. His Secretary of State for Education, Antony Crosland, appointed a Public Schools Commission in the autumn of 1965 'to advise on the best way of integrating the public schools with the State system of education'. Once again, the opponents of the public schools must have believed that the hour had come. Once again they were to be disappointed.

The Public Schools Commission

It was Antony Crosland, the archetypal Gaitskellite and Labour moderate, who insisted that the new government should tackle the problem of the public schools without delay. The public schools thought they were being threatened with abolition by extremists whereas in fact they were being offered a role by the moderates. The Labour left wing had no interest in integrating the public schools in the general education system any more than they had in reforming the House of Lords; until the revolution swept all privilege away, the public schools and the House of Lords served as useful reminders of the need for class struggle.

Crosland wanted the Cabinet to appoint a Royal Commission on the lines of the Clarendon and Taunton Commissions in the 1860s, but the Cabinet refused to pitch the inquiry at that exalted level. Crosland had to be satisfied with a departmental committee. From the start he had difficulty finding suitable members. Five people to whom he offered the chairmanship turned it down. His sixth choice, John Newsom, accepted. Newsom had already chaired one education inquiry, on the education of average and below-average children, whose report had drawn attention to an unsatisfied boarding need.

Some of Newsom's colleagues on the Public Schools Commission did not find him an altogether effective chairman. Some thought him too old, others too complex a character. One described him as almost pathologically vain and a compulsive leaker of information to the press.

Whatever Newsom may have lacked in determination to find a solution to the problem of the public schools was provided by the vice-chairman, David Donnison, the Professor of Social Administration at the London School of Economics. Donnison, who chaired the Commission for the second stage of its work—on the independent day schools—was that familiar English figure, the ex-public school boy who was determined to reform the public schools.

The rest of the team appears to have been appointed to achieve a majority in favour of a solution that would force change on the public schools, particularly in the direction of a comprehensive entry, without going as far as abolition. Crosland interested himself in the choice of particular individuals but he left much of the work of setting up the Commission to his Minister of State at the Department, Reg Prentice.

It was at this point that I made a first, unsuccessful attempt to play a part in public school politics. As a young assistant master at Harrow, I did not trust the headmasters to represent the views of the rank and file. In January 1965 I wrote to Crosland, expressing the hope that these views would not be ignored. Reg Prentice replied. Crosland had asked him to deal with 'questions arising from the Government's policy to bring about the integration of the public schools into the state system of education'. How far, he asked, were my views representative of public school teachers in my age group? He invited me for an informal chat at Curzon Street and I accepted. That he should have been prepared to give time to me and that I should have been received with such kindness, now seems surprising. I was of no importance and had no brief to speak for other teachers. Prentice suggested that many teachers in public schools felt guilty because they were devoting their careers to a small group of privileged children. I said that I thought this was probably true of many of the younger teachers. After the visit I wrote to propose that the membership of the Commission should include an assistant teacher and clumsily hinted that I was the man. Prentice had the good sense to ignore my proposal.

I need not have worried. The two headmasters who were appointed to the Commission—John Dancy of Marlborough and Tom Howarth of St. Paul's—were well qualified to represent the variety of views that existed among those who taught in the public schools. On the face of it, Dancy and Howarth represented the more progressive and more conservative wings of the Headmasters' Conference, though that description does scant justice to two very able individuals.

John Dancy had already acquired a reputation as one of the headmasters who recognized that the public schools had to make changes both in their lifestyle and in their relations with the maintained system. At Marlborough he had abolished the beating of boys by boys. While the Commission was at work, he became the first headmaster to admit girls to the sixth form. In his book *The Public Schools and the Future* he had already explored ways in which public schools could help to meet national needs in education.

A brilliant scholar at Winchester and Oxford, Dancy combined to a marked degree open-mindedness and intellectual rigour. He wanted the Public Schools Commission to succeed. Despite his own dazzling academic career—he had carried off almost every prestigious prize at Oxford—he was prepared to see the public schools move towards an intake that would comprehend all abilities.

Tom Howarth of St. Paul's held the opposite view. Throughout the Commission's deliberations he—almost alone—insisted that, however desirable a greater social mix in the public schools, academic quality should not be diluted. In the Headmasters' Conference, it was John Dancy whose views ran counter to those of his colleagues; *Athenasius contra mundum*, Tom Howarth called him. But in the Commission it was Howarth who played the role of Athenasius. He did it with characteristic wit and a sharp eye for the sillier pretensions of the fashions and gurus of the sixties. 'As I listen to and read the endless flow of educational theorizing about Pestalozzi and Froebel and Neill, and unstreaming and multiple options and, to quote Mr Macarthur of *The Times*, "The School which never says no", all derived from Rousseau,' he told the Headmasters' Conference in 1968, 'I sometimes feel like the great Victorian atheist, W. K. Clifford, who confessed that when listening to the theological disputes of his day he was continually harrassed by a still small voice which whisphered "Fiddlesticks".'

If Howarth's views were reactionary, that was only in relation to the fast-flowing trends of progressive education in the sixties. He was a realist, not a reactionary. He saw himself as a middle-of-the-road man whose heroes were 'Louis Philippe and Kerensky (or in the more noble times More and Falkland)'. He did not deny the need for reform but he was sceptical of the idealistic theories that the reformers espoused so eagerly. He recognized that some aspects of the public schools' lifestyle had outlived their usefulness; one senior member of the Headmasters' Conference thought him a dangerous radical for saying that public schools should place less emphasis on the three traditional compulsions—chapel, cadet corps and cricket. But on the question of academic standards he refused to compromise. In the words of the old Methodist Covenant service, he was 'swimming against the tide, steering contrary to the time'. The tide in the late sixties was running strongly in favour of the abolition of academic selection.

Howarth failed to win over his colleagues on the Commission who rejected his plea for the retention of some selective public schools with high academic standards. The majority view was expressed by W. S. Hill, the headmaster of Myers Grove Comprehensive School in Sheffield, who 'would have none of this because it emphasized the prestigious few, and made the rest feel they did not count'.

The Commission's terms of reference were drawn up in such a way that Howarth's failure was inevitable. On the crucial question of a selective versus a comprehensive intake, the terms of reference gave the Commission no chance to make up its own mind. It was told firmly that it was expected to pay special attention to a number of objectives, including 'to move towards a progressively wide range of academic attainment, so that the public schools sector may increasingly conform with national policy for the maintained sector.' In other words, whatever sort of integration was proposed, the public schools would have to 'go comprehensive'. On this issue conformity, not diversity, was the order.

Not surprisingly, Tom Howarth objected to the terms of reference. In April 1967 he wrote to the chairman of the Commission, 'My real trouble fundamentally is that I find I can subscribe less and less as time goes on to the terms of reference.' He offered to resign from the Commission but was persuaded not to do so. John Dancy also disliked the terms of reference but believed—a little naïvely perhaps—that they could be changed. He told a preparatory school conference in Oxford: 'Before agreeing to serve on the Commission, I asked Mr Crosland whether we would be entitled to reject our terms of reference and recommend something altogether different if that seemed the right thing to do. He assured me we were. Intelligent people would deal with an important problem on no other basis.'

But the Commission showed no willingness to alter the terms of reference. They accepted the comprehensive doctrine. The closest they ever came to flirting with heresy was a half-hearted reference in their recommendations that schools catering entirely for gifted children, while not absolutely excluded, 'should be viewed with considerable caution'. Clearly some members of the Commission were so opposed to what they regarded as academic élitism, that they positively relished the prospect of schools of acknowledged excellence such as Winchester being obliged to open their doors to boys of average and below-average ability.

The terms of reference were much influenced by Michael Young, the Director of the Institute of Community Studies and a member of the Central Advisory Council for Education. Young, who had been educated at Dartington Hall, a 'far-out' progressive boarding school and the very antithesis of the traditional boarding public school, was a keen advocate not only of comprehensive schooling but also of the need to provide boarding education for children who suffered from various types of disadvantage. The terms of reference, therefore, pointed the

Commission both in the direction of a wider social and academic intake and towards the provision of boarding places for children from poorer homes. From the start, the Commission was encouraged to solve the problem of integrating the public schools in the state system in terms of boarding.

Programmed in this way by their terms of reference, the Commission decided to deal with the boarding schools separately from the day schools. This policy was opposed by at least one member of the Commission, John Vaizey, who did not accept that the problem of the public schools could be solved in terms of boarding: he rejected the idea that if you put pupils from a different social class into the beds, the divisiveness of the public schools would disappear. Vaizey wanted the Commission to consider the independent public schools as a whole but once again the majority went their own way. The Commission's First Report, published in 1968, dealt solely with the independent boarding schools.

Given the Commission's conviction that the boarding schools were the nub of the problem and their belief that there was a large, unsatisfied need for boarding among the poorer sections of society, what could be more natural than that the members of the Commission should see the solution to the former in terms of the latter. The discovery of boarding need was a godsend. To meet it by thrusting the needy children on hitherto exclusive schools provided a perfect answer to the question of how to strike a middle course between doing nothing about the public schools and abolishing them.

What was even more convenient was that there was already in hand a research project on boarding education sponsored by the Department of Education and Science. The research was being directed by Dr Royston Lambert, a young sociologist who made his name as an expert on boarding education—which he had never experienced—but who in the seventies passed from a position of educational prominence to one of almost total obscurity. Lambert had founded the Research Unit into Boarding Education in 1964 in the wake of the Martin and Newsom Reports which had drawn attention to certain categories of children who were thought to be in need of boarding education. With the help of Lambert's research, the Commission extended these categories to include almost any case where the circumstances of the home or of the parents' employment indicated that the child's educational development would benefit from boarding. Of the Commission's ten categories of boarding need, the last read: 'Where there are any other exceptional circumstances which severely impede a child's education progress.' With such a wide and imprecise definition of boarding needs it is not surprising that the Commission estimated that the unsatisfied boarding need might be as high as 80,000 children.

The conclusion was obvious. By insisting that the public schools should make approximately half their boarding places available to these children the Commission's various objectives would be achieved. The schools would become more academically comprehensive and less socially divisive. They would cease to be the preserves of the rich. Under the impact of disadvantaged children from poor homes, the schools' lifestyle would have to be reformed and purged of those traditions that most jarred on liberal susceptibilities. And the schools would be integrated without being abolished. How could anyone dissent from this neat and timely solution to a problem that had bedevilled English education and society for so long?

In April 1968, the Commission's First Report was presented to the new Labour Secretary of State, Edward Short, a former headmaster of a maintained secondary school. The Report's recommendations were never discussed in the Cabinet, nor does anyone at any time appear to have regarded them as the basis for political action. Short certainly showed no enthusiasm for them. Like the victim of an epidemic, the Commission's First Report was buried quickly and without ceremony.

The complete failure of the Commission's First Report is not difficult to explain. There was no political capital to be earned by implementing its recommendations. Most of the Labour Party opposed them, particularly the left wing who had no wish to see the schools escape execution by donning egalitarian colours. The Conservative Party opposed the scheme of integration as unnecessary and impracticable. The Liberals agreed that the public schools should be associated more closely with the 'national system' but thought the need for boarding was exaggerated. The local authorities—who would have to meet the bill—and the maintained schools also questioned the existence of widespread boarding need and doubted whether the public schools were anyway the place to send disadvantaged children. Finally, the public school heads on the whole shared Tom Howarth's view that the Commission's insistence that integration must mean that 50 per cent of the schools' intake should be 'assisted children' with an emphasis on broadening the academic level, was too inflexible. In their submission to the Commission, the public schools had said that they were keen to meet the unsatisfied boarding need and to achieve a more socially mixed entry. They wanted to help and to change but on their own terms. They did not want to be changed out of all recognition which is what acceptance of the Commission's recommendations would have meant.

The essential weakness of the Commission's First Report was that it attempted to force a marriage between two problems that looked made for each other but which were in truth incompatible. A marriage between the alleged divisiveness of the public schools and the theoretical boarding need would certainly have been convenient but as the basis for a lasting relationship between the public schools and the state system of education it lacked credibility. As John Vaizey pointed out in his 'note of reservation' to the First Report, the Commission failed to distinguish between boarding need and demand. It was all very well for Dr Lambert's young research team to diagnose various categories of disadvantage and prescribe boarding education as a remedy, but demand for boarding education came almost exclusively from middle-class parents whose motives had little or nothing to do with disadvantage or boarding need. Lambert seems to have imagined that once the parents of the genuinely disadvantaged children appreciated the benefits of boarding and the public schools had undergone a radical change of lifestyle, then boarding need and boarding demand would coincide. It was a donnish theory lacking common sense. As a Liberal Party paper commented, 'A very large proportion of parents do not *want* to send their children away to school, and a child with a broken home may be better off with foster-parents and at a day school than in a boarding school.'

Few people outside the Commission were convinced by Lambert's arguments. Ten years later the whole scheme for meeting boarding need in the context of the public schools has an air of fantasy and it is difficult to understand why it should ever have been seriously proposed.

When the proposal was shelved, some members of the Commission blamed an unholy alliance of the left wing of the Labour Party and the public schools. But there was no need to look for a conspiracy. The recommendations of the Commission's First Report were not assassinated; they died a natural death because they were unworkable.

No doubt this suited the Prime Minister, who could take credit for establishing the Commission but was under no pressure to implement its recommendations. In his own account of his Government's record, Wilson refers briefly to the setting up of the Public Schools Commission but the recommendations are neither mentioned nor discussed.

The Commission now turned its attention to the independent day schools and the direct grant grammar schools. John Newsom handed over the chairmanship to David Donnison and left the Commission. John Dancy and Tom Howarth also left but the newly constituted Commission included three heads of direct grant schools—Bruce McGowan of Solihull, Roger Young of George Watson's, Edinburgh, and Jean Wilks of King Edward VI High School for Girls, Birmingham. It also included C. R. Allison, a former head of Brentwood, an independent day school. These four could be counted on to put the case for academic selection, as Tom Howarth had done.

For this part of its work the Commission was given an additional term of reference which required it to advise on the most effective method by which the direct grant grammar schools could 'participate in the movement towards comprehensive reorganization'. It was a misfortune both for the public schools and for those who wanted to integrate rather than destroy them, that the work of the Commission had to be carried out at a time of educational turmoil, when feelings on the issue of comprehensive versus selective intake to secondary education ran high. As had been the case with its work on the independent boarding schools, the majority on the Commission were determined that integration should mean the end of selection. The minority argued for a few selective integrated schools catering for gifted children but they were no more successful in their advocacy than Tom Howarth had been. The Commission recommended that any independent day schools or direct grant grammar schools that opted to join the state system must become comprehensive in intake.

The direct grant grammar schools (known as grant-aided schools in Scotland) were regarded by the comprehensive lobby as a dangerous anachronism. The idea of the direct grant had been introduced by the Education Act of 1902. The direct grant regulations in force at the time of the Commission required the schools which received the grant to make at least 25 per cent of their places available to pupils from state primary schools and their fees would be paid by the Local Education Authority. The LEA could, if it wished, take more than 25 per cent of the places; in 1968 LEAs were taking up over 50 per cent of places at ninety-three out of the 178 direct grant schools. Those pupils not sponsored by the LEA could nevertheless have their fees remitted on the basis of a means test approved by the Department of Education and Science. In addition, the Department paid a capitation grant for all pupils (with a higher grant for those in the sixth form). In return for this generous financial support, the schools had to accept that one-third of the school governors be appointed by the LEA and that the Secretary of State had the right to approve new buildings and changes in fees.

The direct grant system that had evolved since the beginning of the century was a characteristically British phenomenon: its origin based on pragmatism rather than on some universal principle, its evolution organic, its mode of operation complex, even arcane, its results highly satisfactory. In the early years of the state system, it provided access to the sort of academic, grammar school education that was seldom available in the government's schools. As the state system developed in quality, so the departure of able boys and girls to the direct grant schools was increasingly resented. Once the state system had rejected academic selection, it was clear that the days of the direct grant were numbered.

Socialist critics of the direct grant argued that as long as the schools were allowed to continue, the comprehensive system, denied the most able pupils, would never have a chance to show its worth. The Labour Party also regarded the direct grant schools as socially divisive. Whereas the schools' defenders claimed that their entry was socially comprehensive, the critics pointed to the fact that the schools were predominantly middle class; only one child in thirteen came from a semi-skilled or an unskilled worker's family, while three out of five had fathers in professional or managerial occupations.

Thus schools that had once been regarded as the doorway to opportunity for children from modest homes, not least for many leading socialists from R. H. Tawney to Denis Healey, were now regarded as anachronistic. The academic excellence that had formerly provided a valuable complement to the maintained sector, now presented a threat. There is no doubt that the Labour Party and the supporters of the comprehensive principle on the Commission were logical in their opposition to the direct grant. It made no sense for a society to abolish selection in its maintained schools and then to continue to finance selection in independent schools. Whether the maintained system could afford to lose access to selective schooling for the most able pupils at a time when the comprehensive schools had not proved themselves capable of catering for such children, is more open to debate. But like so many educational debates, it cannot be settled by reference to conclusive evidence. If some comprehensive schools cannot cater for the more able pupils, is this because there is something inherently hostile to high academic standards in the comprehensive idea or because so many of the country's able children have gone to independent and direct grant schools? The unresolved debate will continue for many years.

All but one of the 178 direct grant schools were academically selective. In terms of examination results, the best schools were more successful than the majority of independent schools and than the remaining maintained grammar schools. But the majority on the Commission believed, with the Labour Party, that this academic success could and would be achieved by comprehensive schools once the direct grant schools had been integrated. Yet it was made clear to the Commission and the Labour Party that the majority of direct grant schools, including the most academically powerful such as Manchester Grammar School and King Edward's School, Birmingham, would choose to become fully independent rather than comprehensive. Some of the more able children would find their way into the maintained system but by no means all, while the teachers most experienced in teaching them would remain outside. In the event 119 schools chose independence.

The terms of reference and the majority in favour of ending selection made the Commission's recommendations predictable. The concept of the direct grant was to disappear—the government should no longer fund selective schools. The direct grant grammar schools and the fully independent day schools should be given the option of coming into the comprehensive system as fully maintained schools. If they chose not to do so, they should be free to continue as independent schools. On this latter point the Commission was explicit: 'The legal right of voluntary bodies to provide efficient private education paid for by parents should not be curtailed.'

Unlike the recommendations of the First Report, those of the Second commanded the support of the majority of the Labour Party. The ending of the direct grant in particular was seen both as a logical step for a country that had turned its back on selection and as a step towards a more just and egalitarian society.

The Commission presented its Second Report to the Secretary of State, Edward Short, in January 1970. But in June, before any action was taken on the Report, Harold Wilson called a general election and lost. The Conservatives had a majority of thirty over all other parties and looked set for a period of five, possibly ten years of government. It seemed that for the seventies at least the direct grant and independent schools would be safe from hostile political action.

Labour's Policy 1970–1979

From the point of view of the Labour moderates, the Public Schools Commission had been a flop. In opposition they were forced to rethink their attitudes. If there was no practicable way of integrating the public schools, then even the moderates would have to see abolition as the long-term goal. Just how the public schools were to be abolished was unclear but by 1973 the Labour Party had firmly committed itself to the principle. *Labour's Programme for Britain*, published by the National Executive in that year, drew a distinction between an immediate commitment to 'end the direct grant system' and a commitment in principle: 'Our aim is to abolish fee-paying in schools and to bring all children of compulsory age into the national education system.'

If the commitment in principle sounded vague it was soon given more precise form by the Party's new spokesman on education, Roy Hattersley. At the annual conference in Cambridge of preparatory school headmasters, he stated bluntly his Party's 'serious intention initially to reduce and eventually to abolish private education in this country'.

Hattersley's speech provoked an outcry. It was as though it had never occurred to anyone that Labour might wish to get rid of the public schools. The press was almost unanimous in condemning his proposals. *The Times* described them as 'a startling trespass on individual liberty'. The *Guardian* had more sympathy with the general principle but accused Hattersley of giving a misleading urgency and precision to a policy that was at best a long-term goal. 'It will also have raised the blood pressure of many who support his general thesis,' the paper's leader commented, 'but have heard it all before and do not any longer believe that Mr Hattersley's reforms will move at anything like the pace he suggests.'

Hattersley's speech brought him considerable publicity and some notoriety. Critics saw him as an ambitious politician anxious to make a name for himself and to win support among the party's rank and file when the annual conference met in Blackpool the following month. But the speech was more thoughtful than the immediate reaction would suggest. He made out a reasoned case against the independent schools which was based on three arguments: the schools were socially divisive; they diverted energy and enthusiasm from the improvement of the education system as a whole; and they consumed a disproportionate share of scarce resources. He rejected the Public Schools Commission's evidence on boarding need and he denied that parental freedom of choice was an absolute right that should never be restricted in the interests of the common good.

Hattersley went on to attempt an analysis of how the disappearance of the private sector could be accomplished. It may have been premature, even imprudent to spell out a detailed programme for abolition, but he wanted to convince his audience that the Labour Party was serious in its intention. After Hattersley the independent schools could never complain that they had not been warned.

'It must be said for Mr Roy Hattersley,' said *The Times* leader, 'that he made no bones about it.' The campaign against the independent sector was outlined step by step to his silent audience. The direct grant would be abolished as the Public Schools Commission had recommended. Then a Labour Government would remove the financial advantages enjoyed by independent schools and by the parents who patronized them, including the schools' status as charities and the parents' ability to treat the children's income separately for tax purposes. The next step would be to restrict or remove altogether the power of local authorities to take up places in independent schools. A more stringent system of inspection before independent schools were recognized as efficient would then be used to weed out the weaker brethren.

These measures would not, as Hattersley acknowledged, damage the more prestigious boys' public schools but the measures would make them more exclusive and isolated; the removal of the undergrowth would expose the enormities of privilege more clearly to the public view. Once the Great Schools had been isolated, abolition would be that much easier. 'Their end could come in many forms,' Hattersley warned, in language rather more suited to one of Ian Fleming's villains. A Bill prohibiting the charging of fees for full-time education was the method of execution he favoured. 'But whilst the method we will wish to use for the final step is more than the choice of detail, in terms of the eventual outcome it is a great deal less important than the existence of political will. I hope I have demonstrated that the political will exists.'

After the first somewhat violent reaction, the independent schools were inclined to believe that Hattersley had not intended them to take him seriously or that he had spoken without the Shadow Cabinet's authority and had overstepped the mark. 'It is difficult to believe that a mature politician should make a proposal that is only worthy of an "angry young man",' three independent-school headmistresses wrote to *The Times*.

But Roy Hattersley had not been speaking for himself alone and had had every intention that his audience should take him seriously. Education policy in the Labour Party is formulated by the National Executive's Science and Education Sub-Committee. The chairman of this sub-committee in the mid-seventies was Joan Lestor, M.P. for Eton and Slough and a prominent left-winger. At the Blackpool conference she re-iterated the policy Hattersley had outlined at Cambridge.

Hattersley contented himself with a few comments on the reaction to his Cambridge speech: 'Of course to talk about equality will produce an immediate howl from the educational establishment. The letter columns of *The Times* will be jammed again. We will have to accept that with rejoicing. The public schools have proved over the last months how desperately hard they will fight to keep an education system that perpetuates their view of how society ought to be. We have to fight just as hard for an education system which will build the sort of society the Labour Party was founded to bring about.'

It was Joan Lestor's task to convince the conference, as Hattersley had tried to convince his audience in Cambridge, that this time the Labour Party meant business. She underlined the Party's pledge to end the direct grant and to make a start on the removal of the tax concessions enjoyed by the independent schools. Abolition could not be brought about tomorrow but the Party was unequivocally committed to it as a long-term aim:

I have told you, comrades, that one of the things we want to look at is the way of dealing with the financial concessions that are in this sector. When my working party looked at this sector we recognized that year after year the Conference, with its hand on its heart, pledged itself to abolish the independent sector of education and did nothing about it. We decided that we would either come back to you and say we were sorry it was not on or we would find ways of doing it. . . . I cannot promise you this morning that we shall be able to take over the top twenty-five of the main public schools of this country. It would not be right for me to make that commitment but that is our long-term commitment: to abolish privilege in education, be it in the state sector or be it in the field of education labelled 'independent'.

The Party's policy was clear. In the words of the Party's *Notes for Speakers*, issued early in 1974, 'The public schools must go, by a process of gradual reduction and eventual abolition.' This has remained the framework for Labour policy ever since, with the emphasis increasingly on the gradual reduction rather than on the eventual abolition.

For the general election in February 1974, the Labour Manifesto committed the Party only to the next step in gradualism: 'All forms of tax relief and charitable status of public schools will be withdrawn.' The election brought Labour back to power with a minority government. When, in the autumn, Wilson called another election and won an overall majority of three, he declared his party's intention of governing for a full five years. The seventies that had looked so safe for independent schools now threatened to witness the first steps in Labour's campaign of reduction.

The first signs were not altogether unfavourable for the independent schools. Labour's 'wafer-thin' majority might discourage even a step as comparatively uncontroversial as the ending of the direct grant. Wilson's appointment of Reg Prentice rather than Roy Hattersley as Secretary of State for Education and Science provided further satisfaction for the independent sector. 'He is not violently anti-public school,' reported John Izbicki of the *Daily Telegraph*, 'he certainly bears nothing like the loathing of the independent sector displayed by Mr Roy Hattersley.'

Prentice was on the right wing of the Party (two years later he was to cross the floor and join the Conservatives) and he had a reputation for down-to-earth good sense rather than radical reform. If he did not exactly inspire confidence among independent schools, he seemed to be a man with whom it would be possible to do business. But if independent schools expected Prentice to soft-pedal Labour's education policy they were soon disappointed. Whatever his personal dislike of the left wing of the Party, Prentice did not hesitate to implement policies that the left wing had advocated—the imposition of universal comprehensive education by law and the abolition of the direct grant. These policies represented one of the few areas on which the two wings of the Labour Party could agree. Prentice said he was in favour of 'a more just and egalitarian society'. In his view, the direct grant created inequalities. The Party was correct therefore in bringing it to an end.

The formal announcement was made early in 1975: during the next academic year direct grant schools would be given the chance of going comprehensive in the maintained sector or of foregoing their grant and choosing independence. When the annual conference came round again Joan Lestor could report with satisfaction that the first step in the long campaign to get rid of privilege in education had been taken.

For the Labour Party it was a relief that at last they had been able to make some progress towards their publicly espoused goal of abolishing the independent sector. The fact that by removing the direct grant they had created in one year more fully independent schools than had been created in any previous century did not concern them. They did not see this as a strengthening of the independent sector but as a postponement of the day of reckoning. Like soldiers retreating to a second line of defence, the direct grant schools that chose independence would soon find that their new position could also be attacked.

That attack, as Hattersley's speech had forecast, began with an attempt to remove the schools' financial and tax concessions. Joan Lestor told the 1975 annual conference, 'I believe that if we set our sights to do something about curtailing the financial concessions that go to certain sections of independent education, we shall begin on the long road that I believe in and this party believes in, and that is the decline and ultimate abolition of the private sector.'

Curtailing the financial concessions proved much more difficult than the Labour Party had anticipated. As charities the schools were exempt from income tax on profits, capital gains and capital transfer tax; and they enjoyed 50 per cent relief on rates. There was widespread political agreement that the concept of charity should be redefined but no one could find a way of disentangling Eton and Winchester from the Royal National Lifeboat Institution and Dr Barnado's Homes. Two high-powered committees—one chaired by Harold Wilson's lawyer, Lord Goodman, the other an expenditure sub-committee of the House of Commons—failed to come up with a solution. In 1977 Labour's National Executive was forced to admit in its report to conference that while the party was still trying to identify a means of removing charitable status from independent schools 'this seems unlikely to produce an easy solution, as the taxation system does not distinguish between charities we would and would not wish to support.' For the two more years of Labour government, the Party's education spokesmen continued to hold out to their supporters some hope of being able to sort out the charity muddle so that the 'genuine will be divided from the privileged', but no formula for action emerged.

Frustrated in this part of the campaign against education privilege, Labour turned its attention to another vulnerable point in the independent schools' defences. There were many pupils in independent schools whose fees were wholly or partly paid by local authorities or by central government. In 1979 ISIS put the number of such pupils at 19,000 or about 6 per cent of the total in independent schools. The funding of these pupils, which was distinct from the direct grant arrangements, was justified on a variety of grounds from local political whim to the obvious boarding need of children of diplomatic and Service personnel. Hattersley had advocated that the local authorities' ability to take up places in independent schools should at least be curtailed. In 1976 this curtailment was achieved by requiring local authorities to seek the approval of the Secretary of State before taking up independent school places; this approval would only be given if there was 'a demonstrable absolute shortage of suitable places in the LEA's schools'. But when it came to the point, the Labour Secretary of State approved 80 per cent of the applications in 1977–8. An attempt to discourage diplomatic and Service personnel from using independent schools was even less successful; the generous boarding allowance enjoyed by diplomats and commissioned officers serving overseas was regarded as an integral part of their remuneration and neither the Foreign Office nor the Ministry of Defence was prepared to see this disturbed for the sake of hitting the independent schools.

In October 1976, Harold Wilson's successor as Labour Prime Minister, James Callaghan, shifted the emphasis of the government's educational policy away from egalitarianism at all costs and on to day-to-day realities of the classroom. His speech at Ruskin College, Oxford, was carefully designed to launch a public debate on the way in which primary and secondary education was being conducted. It was a sensible political move to check the mounting public criticism of poor results and bad discipline in some of the new comprehensive schools. The 'Great Debate' was orchestrated by the new Secretary of State, Shirley Williams.

It was fortunate for the Labour Party and for the country's

schools that a politician of Shirley Williams' calibre was prepared to take on what must have seemed a thankless task, in an office that has never commanded much political influence or public esteem. Her intelligence, realism and lack of bigotry brought to the battered ranks of the education service a new sense of direction and purpose. She raised morale by the simple yet sincere device of being enthusiastic. She had the stamina and patience to listen to all shades of opinion and the courage to make up her mind. She was the only Secretary of State for Education since the war to make a major public impact and if disenchantment set in before the end of her term of office, it says much for her that in an unglamorous post she had been able to generate any enchantment at all.

When she addressed the Party's annual conference for the first time as Secretary of State she set her speech in an unemotional key: ideals must be grounded in the reality of present resources. She made no reference to the independent schools. Her approach to this contentious issue was severely practical. She wanted to see the schools disappear but she acknowledged that there was no quick or easy method of achieving this. Labour's policy should therefore be to concentrate on improving the maintained sector. The headmasters of independent schools, who as a group are peculiarly susceptible to feminine charm, were tempted to regard her as an ally. But her opposition to independent schools was no less implacable than that of previous Labour ministers; it was just more honest and realistic.

As the life of Callaghan's government drew to a close, the independent schools sensed that a long period of political challenge was ending. The Conservatives appeared likely to win the next election. Popular opinion, in so far as it could be identified, was much less hostile to independent schools than it had been fifteen years before. The press and the other media were generally sympathetic. The schools themselves were confident and full. When the April 1979 election produced a comfortable Conservative majority, the heads of independent schools experienced a feeling of relief, tinged with self-congratulation. They had survived.

4

Response to the Political Challenge

Improving Public Relations

Public school headmasters are political animals. Whatever other qualities of intellect and character they possess and however much they consciously or unconsciously disguise the political aspect of their nature, success in their jobs requires qualities that we would recognize as political—stamina, an instinct for survival, a polite ruthlessness, a shrewd judgement of men and opportunities and a flair for identifying and, if need be, diverting the currents of popular opinion. To win the support of pupils, masters, parents, governors and old boys simultaneously requires a high degree of political dexterity.

These political qualities are not immediately obvious. But the façade is misleading. The conventional, even bland, exterior usually hides an astute political brain; indeed if it does not the headmaster is unlikely to survive for long. Those public school headmasters whose careers have crashed have usually been guilty not of incompetence or immorality, but of political clumsiness.

In 1964, when Labour came to power with the explicit intention of dealing with the public schools, the question was how far the headmasters' political acumen could be transposed from the small world of the school to the wider political field in which their schools were threatened. Above all it was crucial that these autocratic men should be prepared to work not only with each other, but also with the headmasters of preparatory schools and with the headmistresses of the girls' independent schools. And before that was achieved a number of well-established prejudices would have to be overcome.

In a political fight for survival, the strength and weakness of the independent sector was the Headmasters' Conference. The 210 boys' public schools represented on the Conference were not all well known but they included all the wealthy and prestigious schools. Any attempt to organize a co-ordinated defence against a hostile government would be crippled if these Great Schools did not throw the weight of their influence behind the project.

But the prestige and wealth of the famous public schools could also be a source of weakness to the independent sector. Secure in their great traditions, these schools might be too proud to join a defensive league constituted in the main of schools of which they had never heard. On their part, the less well-known schools, particularly the smaller preparatory and girls' schools, might fear that the famous schools would call the tune and have little understanding of the problems of their less well-endowed allies.

The same problem had arisen a hundred years before when Edward Thring, the headmaster of Uppingham, had organized a defensive league of headmasters to oppose the recommendations of an earlier government commission on independent schools. At the first meeting of this defensive league, or Headmasters' Conference as it became known, in December 1869, the famous schools were noticeable by their absence. The headmasters of Eton, Winchester, Westminster, Rugby, St. Paul's and Harrow had been invited but did not turn up. There was so little belief in the necessity of co-operation that of seventy headmasters invited only twelve came. One headmaster wrote to Thring: 'I doubt on the whole whether I shall ever be able to attend the proposed meetings, so strongly do I value the perfect rest of the holidays and the privilege of complete independence in dealing with . . . such educational difficulties as may arise.'

Those headmasters who did attend displayed precisely that ambivalence towards the Great Schools that characterized the first moves towards unity in the independent sector in the 1960s and 1970s. Dr Pears of Repton thought the Conference should try hard to get the Great Schools to co-operate; he longed for 'a great name to help the Conference along'. But John Mitchinson, the robust northerner who was headmaster of King's School, Canterbury, took the opposite view: 'If they think isolation a benefit, we cannot help it, and we are not dependent in our work and present object upon the prestige which the names would give us. . . . I most certainly object to being tied to the chariot wheels of the Great Schools.'

In a few years all the Great Schools had joined the Conference. They did not dominate the Conference as much as Mitchinson had feared, though they did provide more than their fair share of chairmen and committee members. The heads of the more prestigious schools also tended to form the core of the informal dining clubs, such as The Twenty-Seven and The Gang, which in a characteristically English way created an inner, charmed circle and made those who were excluded suspect that it was here that the effective decisions were taken.

By the early 1960s, suspicion and envy of the Great Schools could still be found in some parts of the independent sector and was one of the problems that would have to be overcome if a new and wider defensive league incorporating all recognized independent schools was to be organized successfully.

Harold Wilson's Labour Government came to power in 1964. It was eight years before the independent schools launched their first co-operative effort in defence, the Independent Schools Information Service, and ten years before the Independent Schools Joint Committee was formed to present a united front on policy. This delayed reaction to political challenge was only partly the result of the difficulty in getting the various groups and interests to work together. There were other lessons to be learned, principal among them being the value and limitations of public relations.

It would be wrong to assume that before this time, independent schools had been unaware of the need to project a favourable image and to counter public criticism. The heads of independent schools, by the very nature of their jobs, have always had to deal with popular, even malicious, misconceptions about their schools. They run what their opponents like to call 'commercial schools' and in the market place unfavourable publicity can mean loss of trade. The oscillating fortunes of the Great Schools in the eighteenth and nineteenth centuries reflected the degree of success or failure with which headmasters built the schools' reputation. Even Dr Arnold had to cope with scathing criticism of his disciplinary methods in the *Northampton Herald*, but when he had established his own reputation and the school's, parents rushed to send their sons to Rugby. In the same century, Westminster's reputation suffered an almost catastrophic decline because the headmaster and governing body failed to respond with energy to the threat of the encroaching city; when the newspapers reported that boys were dying in insanitary conditions, parents were disinclined to send their sons.

Even in the twentieth century, when public schools' fortunes followed a more even course, a successful headmaster could transform a school's reputation and a weak or incompetent one could damage it, if not beyond repair, then certainly for many years. A man like Canon Shirley built the modern reputation of King's School, Canterbury, partly because he had a flair for public relations that bordered on the unscrupulous. But by the early 1960s the art of public relations had developed to a point at which it was increasingly unwise for an amateur to chance his arm without professional guidance. Headmasters had always had to deal with an inquisitive press but now television, both national and local, presented a new and unfamiliar challenge. With a more hostile political climate and a more sophisticated and demanding media, the heads of independent schools were forced to swallow their distaste for the concept of professional public relations.

It was characteristic of the headmasters of the boys' preparatory schools that they should have been the first to appoint a public relations sub-committee and to sign a contract with a firm of public relations consultants. Britain's preparatory schools are a modern phenomenon; 90 per cent were founded in the hundred years from 1850 to 1950. As their name suggests, they exist to prepare boys—and more recently girls—for entry to the public schools at the age of thirteen. There are 441 boys' preparatory schools in membership of IAPS, some of which now admit girls, and 130 prep schools for girls only. When the Labour Government came to power in 1964, only a quarter of the boys' prep schools were non-profit-making charitable trusts with properly constituted governing bodies. The majority were owned by the headmaster or by a private company. Since 1964 the change from private ownership to charitable trust has accelerated so that it is now the majority of headmasters who enjoy the security of a proper contract and salary and the support of a board of trustees or governors. But the spirit of self-reliance lives on.

The heads of prep schools are perhaps more varied than those of public schools. Some are backwoodsmen whose educational outlook belongs to the pre-war period. Others are refreshingly free from the conservatism and complacency that sometimes afflicts the heads of the public schools. Few can now afford to ignore educational trends or to take a detached view of sales techniques. They are in the market place with a vengeance. With schools that are seldom large enough to be economically viable— three-quarters have fewer than 200 pupils—the heads have had to be more resourceful than their public school colleagues.

The Incorporated Association of Preparatory Schools (IAPS) has always been quicker than the Headmasters' Conference (HMC) to respond to changes in the political, economic and educational climate. Its origins make an intriguing contrast to Thring's first meeting of 'very superior men' at Uppingham in 1869. On a March afternoon in 1892 seven prep school headmasters met in a waiting room at Marylebone Station to discuss the size of cricket ball to be used in inter-school matches. This unpretentious and practical discussion set the tone for the organization it had unwittingly started.

It is not surprising, therefore, that in 1957, at a time when most public school headmasters still regarded public relations as a hardly respectable activity, IAPS started to explore the advantages of retaining a public relations consultant. It was five years before HMC followed their example. In 1962, HMC appointed an individual public relations consultant and a year later revamped its not very effective Publicity Committee as a Public

Relations Sub-Committee. The Conservative Government would have to go to the country in November 1964 at the latest and the prospect of a Labour government after thirteen years of Conservative rule overcame the public schools' antipathy to professionalism in their public relations.

In April 1963 their new consultant advised them on the first steps to be taken:

> I believe that now is the time to take more positive action in providing the public with a straightforward and up-to-date picture of the public schools. In my view the matter of first importance (and urgency) is the collection and collation of factual information on all aspects of HMC education. The lack of such a 'Brief' is a serious handicap not only in refuting the published arguments of critics but also in initiating positive action. . . . Possibly this autumn, almost certainly next spring or summer, there will be a General Election preceded by an immense amount of loose talk, catch-phrases and arguments based on emotion rather than realities—and emanating from all Parties—on the subject of education. Against this, information from the Brief should provide an effective counter.

He also advised them that the Brief should answer the most common criticisms of the public schools: that they were divisive, privileged, expensive and still addicted to corporal punishment.

The newly constituted Public Relations Sub-Committee welcomed these proposals and prepared to act on them. For the next AGM the subjects chosen should 'show the contribution of public schools to the nation', and one session should be devoted to a discussion of the new universities 'to help counter the idea that public schools thought only in terms of Oxford and Cambridge'. Meanwhile, research should be promoted at once to procure accurate and comprehensive factual details about public schools. The sub-committee also proposed that a 'trade magazine' should be started as a forum for the exchange of ideas and to show a wider audience how different public school reality was from the unfavourable image.

The Chairman of the Sub-Committee was John Carleton, the headmaster of Westminster, and the members included a number of men, such as Alan Barker of They Leys and Frank Fisher of St. Edward's, Oxford, who proved astute operators in the public relations field. From the start Frank Fisher was the moving spirit. The second son of Archbishop Geoffrey Fisher and one of the very few bachelor headmasters, Fisher had his father's grasp of administration, together with a mind open to new ideas and a talent for getting things done. He bothered about detail without ever letting himself become immersed in it. In the period we are considering, 1964–79, he was probably the most influential headmaster on the Conference. Others may have caught the public eye or initiated important changes in policy, but Fisher's presence for so long at the centre of HMC affairs was a decisive factor in the modernization of HMC's attitude to politics and public relations. It was he who proposed and launched the trade magazine *Conference* and who started the Political Sub-Committee in 1973. He was for a time Chairman of the Public Relations Sub-Committee and in 1973 Chairman of the Conference. In 1979 he became Chairman of the ISJC's Advisory Committee which had been started by Desmond Lee, an equally skilled administrator, and which has developed into the 'think-tank' for independent education.

The presence of Fisher and other capable men did not prevent the sub-committee getting off to a bad start. Their chairman invited a distinguished educationalist, Alec Peterson, the Director of the Oxford University Department of Education, to undertake the factual research on public schools that had been recommended. The HMC Committee endorsed the choice but when it was put to the full Conference at its AGM, someone pointed out that Peterson was a member of the Liberal Party. The invitation was promptly withdrawn. Peterson was understandably annoyed and critical. He argued that the research would carry more weight if the public knew it had been carried out by someone whose political sympathies were not identical with those of most public school headmasters, a point that the Conference seems to have overlooked.

This incident, of no great importance in itself, underlined how sensitive, even paranoid, the public schools were about any factual information falling into unfriendly hands. As Peterson pointed out, it was just as well the left-wing press did not discover that HMC was not willing to let a Liberal undertake their research. But the embarrassing withdrawal of this invitation had one useful consequence. The Conference was now determined that whoever was asked to undertake the research, the control of its use and publication must remain in HMC's own hands.

In the event the research was done by Graham Kalton, a lecturer in social statistics at the London School of Economics, who had been recommended by a sound Conservative source.

Kalton's admirably dispassionate survey was published in 1966, just in time to be of use to the Public Schools Commission. Though it was the first comprehensive factual survey of HMC schools, it was not as complete as Kalton would have wished. Eton refused to complete the questionnaire that would have revealed the exact extent of the College's wealth. Other governing bodies appear to have jibed at this part of the inquiry and one or two schools had to be pressed hard to take part in the research at all. Nevertheless as a factual account of the schools it went a long way to meet the original aim, 'to inform ourselves, to feed into the streams of public opinion and to be prepared in any future emergency'.

Labour's victory in 1964 and the appointment of the Public Schools Commission had brought a new note of urgency to HMC's public relations effort. In July 1965, Alan Barker had taken over the chairmanship of the sub-committee. A former Cambridge history don and Eton master, Barker enjoyed provoking his more socially conscious colleagues with the expression of robust right-wing opinions. He was a flamboyant figure, concerned that the public schools should align themselves unequivocally with the Conservative Party, yet not afraid to tell the Swinton Conservative College that in his view the Tories had failed to 'give any help in making the public schools of more use to the community as a whole'. A Tory radical, he was as impatient with the caution of HMC as he was with the impetuous haste with which the state system was embracing progressive theories.

It fell to Barker to end HMC's contract with the individual public relations consultant who had advised the Conference since 1962 and to select a major public relations firm whose greater resources would be essential at a critical period. This step was taken in the summer of 1967. It was none too soon. The Public Schools Commission was expected to produce its first report early the following year and had already allowed much of the evidence that was hostile to public schools to be published. 'Since January all sorts of bodies, including the NUT and TUC, have been airing their views about public schools,' one headmaster wrote anxiously to Barker, 'and nobody has made any reply.'

The much greater financial outlay required to retain a major public relations firm had to be met by individual schools, which meant in practice that the scheme had to be approved by 210 governing bodies. But governors were not prepared to give headmasters a free hand with public relations. As one senior member of the Governing Bodies Association (GBA) put it at the time: 'As you probably know, many governing bodies regard headmasters as dangerous left-wing radicals to whom nothing can safely be entrusted, and if we are to keep the governing bodies in line it is essential that the Governing Bodies Association be seen to be sharing in the control operation.'

That headmasters who, by and large, were conservative both in instinct and political conviction should have been regarded as 'dangerous left-wing radicals' was an indication of how far to the right some members of governing bodies were. When headmasters are criticized for not moving faster towards, for example, a more constructive relationship with the maintained system, it is often forgotten that in some—though by no means all—cases their freedom of manoeuvre is severely restricted by the attitude of their governors.

On the issue of public relations, governors clearly did not trust headmasters. The activities of the public relations firm were to be controlled by a joint committee of governors and headmasters, an arrangement that might have cramped the style of the professionals had the members of the committee not been themselves so wholeheartedly convinced of the need for public schools to adopt a more positive and outward-looking stance. The governors included Sir William Hayter, a Fellow of Winchester and Warden of New College, Sir Robert Birley who had just retired as headmaster of Eton and Kirkpatrick Young, a governor of Shrewsbury and a key figure in the creation of ISIS in 1972; on the headmasters' side were Alan Barker, Frank Fisher, Tom Howarth and Donald Lindsay, the headmaster of Malvern who was to become the first Director of ISIS.

For five years, until their public relations effort was absorbed into that of ISIS in October 1972, the boys' public schools were the effective defenders of the independent sector. The prep schools, though first to enter the public relations field, tended to confine their effort to the protection of their own position. As for the girls' schools, their headmistresses were even more suspicious of public relations than the headmasters and did not agree to set up a public relations committee until 1973.

It is difficult to say how much the public schools and the public relations consultants achieved in this period. The transformation of the public schools image and their confident and sophisticated handling of the media belong to the years following the establishment of ISIS in 1972. But the five previous years had laid the foundations of public relations expertise and had helped to convince the doubters in the independent sector that there were positive benefits to be had from professional help. Attacks on public schools in the press were quickly answered; information was provided for politicians and journalists who were disposed to be favourable; above all, the public schools themselves, by going into the public arena and being prepared to give as good as they got, not only gained in confidence but also won the respect of many people whose attitude towards them was at best neutral. The accusation that public schools were too tentative in their own defence carried much less conviction in 1972 than it had in 1967.

The main business of these years was to deal with the Public Schools Commission. Here policy and public relations overlapped and many of those involved in the latter were also involved in drafting the joint GBA/HMC Submission of evidence to the Commission. Because we can now see how ineffective the Commission was and what a negligible threat it posed to the independent public schools, it is tempting to dismiss as exaggerated the fears of many headmasters that their schools were likely to be sentenced, if not to execution, then at least to a permanent loss of freedom. As will happen with men awaiting sentence, some were inclined to co-operate with the authorities while others remained defiant. Some of the co-operators were opportunists but there were a few who would have endorsed John Dancy's line and accepted the recommendations of the First Report. It is perhaps as well that their sincerity was not put to the test because whatever the headmasters' personal views, few governing bodies would have accepted integration unless the alternative was tantamount to abolition.

For those drafting the Submission, the problem was not so much how to reflect the diversity of views in the Conference but how to oppose, without appearing merely obstructive, the underlying assumptions in the Commission's terms of reference: that the schools were socially divisive and that academic selection was anathema. Their *Joint Submission to the Public Schools Commission* is therefore in two parts: first a carefully argued refutation of the charges of divisiveness and privilege, then a series of constructive proposals on how the public schools could contribute to the national education needs.

The Submission claimed that a more socially mixed entry, with no boy prevented from coming 'merely because his parents are not well enough off to pay the fees', was 'something that many of us have long hoped for'. As for a comprehensive academic entry the schools could not individually cover the whole range of academic achievement but the independent sector as a whole could, and this would surely meet the Government's expressed wish to see the public schools 'move towards a progressively wider range of academic attainment'. The schools agreed with the Commission that it was right 'to begin with boarding'. They denied that they were so inflexibly middle class that they could not adapt to children from poorer homes and they declared themselves willing to participate in any sensible scheme that would enable them to meet the country's boarding need.

The schools took a more realistic view of boarding need than the Commission and did not make the mistake of confusing need with demand. 'As we are not Approved Schools,' the Submission commented drily, 'even those sent to us on grounds of need would have to be sent with the active co-operation of their parents.' But the schools shared with the Commission a conviction that there was in Britain a large, unfulfilled need for boarding education. It is true that more than one government report had identified such a need but it is hard not to escape the conclusion that much of the talk of boarding need in the 1960s was a question of fashion. Not much was heard of the need in the seventies—on the contrary, the maintained system was running down its boarding provision.

It is easy enough to think of theoretical arguments why a child's schooling might be more successful in a residential situation, but in the great majority of advanced societies boarding is thought appropriate only in the most extreme cases of disadvantage or geographical remoteness. In Britain it is a matter of tradition rather than need, but it was understandable that men who ran boarding schools and who were themselves the products of such schools should have told the Commission that 'boarding education is almost essential for many and for a great many others desirable.'

Thus the public schools were a further encouragement to the Commission to solve the problem of integration in terms of boarding. When the Labour Party Conference in 1968 dismissed the Commission's recommendations on boarding out of hand, the chairmen of GBA and HMC, Sir William Hayter and Donald Lindsay, wrote to *The Times* to express their disappointment. 'We hope this very negative decision is not a prelude to that guerrilla war against the Public Schools which the Commission itself very properly deplores in its report.'

Was the public schools' disappointment genuine? At the end of their Submission they had said: 'In conclusion we would like to remind the Commission of the difficulties with which we have been beset in this matter since the war. On the one hand, we have been told that there was no need to do anything—we were doing very well as we were; on the other hand, any suggestions for action which we have made have been dismissed as face-saving gestures.'

Their critics, including those in the Labour Party, thought their interest in the boarding needs of poorer children was another face-saving gesture. With so many individual head-masters and different types of school involved, it is impossible to know for certain whether or not the critics were right in their cynicism. But it is important to consider the question because the expressed desire of the public schools to admit pupils regardless of background has been a recurring theme over the last fifty years.

The schools' claim to be sincere was supported by the fact that the 1942 Fleming Committee on the Public Schools was set up by the President of the Board of Education *at the express wish* of GBA and HMC, 'both of which,' the Committee reported, 'had been considering for some time previously by what means the Schools which they represented could be of service to a wider range of pupils.' Schools which had no intention of opening their doors more widely would hardly have urged the Government to set up a Committee to achieve this end. The failure of the Fleming Committee's proposals could not be blamed on the public schools which continued to press for a scheme of association with the state system well into the 1950s. Individual headmasters, such as Robert Birley, who had been a member of the Fleming Committee, argued consistently that it was essential for the public schools to come in from the cold.

But the 1966 Public Schools Commission, appointed by a political party openly hostile to the schools, was bound to produce a more cautious response from the headmasters. The latter wanted to make a deal with Labour, not least because that would enable them to forget politics and return to the job of education, but they did not want to change too much, too fast. They wanted to have their cake and eat it; integration and independence, a wider social mix but business as usual. They wanted the threat of abolition to be removed but they did not want to have to pay too high a price. Their attitude to what the Commission proposed was, therefore, ambivalent rather than insincere.

The Beginning of ISIS: a Step towards Unity

The Conservative election victory in June 1970, following so soon after the stillbirth of the Commission's Report on the Boarding Schools, gave the independent schools a breathing space in which to reflect on the future. Neither integration nor the abolition of the direct grant was now an immediate danger. But as so often happens the removal of a threat provided an opportunity for self-analysis and self-criticism. There was a suspicion in the independent sector that the challenge of the Public Schools Commission had not been handled well. There had been a characteristic disagreement between GBA and HMC about whether their evidence to the Commission would be published. The Public School Bursars Association (PSBA) was angry that it had not been represented on the Joint Committee that had drafted the evidence. Above all, it was felt that the independent sector needed a stronger and more professional central organization that could speak with authority for *all* independent schools. Even before the June election, the chairman of the PSBA, W. G. Jack, the Bursar of Uppingham, had sent a strongly worded memorandum to Walter Hamilton, the chairman of GBA:

> It seems extraordinary to this observer that an 'industry' of the size indicated in the opening paragraph of this paper i.e. the independent schools should have such weak administration. Admitting that independent schools, as their name implies, have separate identities and needs, nevertheless they constitute a coherent whole, with a multitude of common aims and needs.

Jack wanted the independent schools to create their own equivalent of the CBI, with sufficient 'authority and weight to negotiate with Governments', formulate policy and 'achieve prompt, accurate and co-ordinated publicity'. Jack's was one of a number of voices advocating a strong central organization but his memorandum of May 1970 appears to have been the one to set the long process in motion.

Bursars are practical men responsible for the financial management of independent schools. Their position in the chain of command is often ambiguous—responsible both to the headmaster and to the governing body. This ambiguity has not infrequently led to conflict between headmasters and bursars, conflict that has sometimes been resolved by the headmaster's departure. Governing bodies tend to regard this constitutional ambiguity as not without advantages; the bursar serves the headmaster but also acts as a brake on his more extravagant schemes. In the major schools such conflict is rare: the governors trust the headmaster and let him get on with the job. But in some of the smaller schools and in particular in the girls' schools, governors sometimes act as though they had no confidence in the ability of academics to understand the financial implications of policy; in these schools the bursar is seen not only as the financial watchdog but also as the one person who is aware of life's realities. In no school is the bursar's role an easy one to fill. Tact, finesse and a thick skin are required. Teachers as a group are inclined to think that they know how to manage the school's finances and they do not hesitate to put their expertise at the disposal of the bursar.

It is hardly surprising therefore that there should have been from time to time friction between the PSBA and the organizations representing headmasters and headmistresses. As far as policy for public schools was concerned, HMC was reluctant to admit the bursars to the discussions; just as bursars believed that few headmasters understood finance, so headmasters believed that few bursars understood education. But as the more aware headmasters and bursars recognized, this was a false dichotomy: education was the service the schools were selling; the quality of education and of financial administration were interdependent.

There was also disagreement between headmasters and bursars on the purpose that a central organization should serve. Headmasters thought in terms of a co-ordinated effort on the political and public relations front; bursars believed that the principal threat was economic not political and wanted the central organization to provide effective financial and legal expertise and initiative. In the early seventies, it was the headmasters' view which prevailed, that is to say that a central public relations and information service should precede any attempt to bring all independent schools under one central policy body on the lines of the CBI. Quite apart from other considerations, the headmasters believed that public relations and information was the only basis on which the various groups in the independent sector could be persuaded to work together.

The argument for starting with a co-ordinated information service was strengthened by the existence of a number of regional centres, each going under the name of 'independent schools information service', which brought together the heads of the public and preparatory schools in the area to promote their schools and disseminate information to prospective customers. The idea had been originated in 1969 by—predictably—a prep school headmaster, John Singleton, of St. John's-on-the-Hill, Chepstow and Colin Mann, the preparatory schools' public relations consultant. In September 1970, GBA began to build on this idea. The two men who provided the leadership in GBA at this stage were Walter Hamilton and Desmond Lee. Both had been headmasters—Hamilton at Westminster and Rugby, Lee at Clifton and Winchester—and both therefore were well placed to understand the delicate negotiations that would be required to convince the heads of schools so different in aims, size, wealth and prestige that there was something to be gained from co-operation.

It was a daunting task. The essence of the independent sector is competition and behind the gentlemanly façade the competition can be cut-throat. Friends and neighbours are also rivals. While no headmaster would gladly see another independent school go under, he may sometimes recall de Rochefoucauld's maxim, 'In the misfortune of our best friends, we find something which is not displeasing to us.' His first duty is to see that his own school is full; if he is confident of doing that, his interest in a national information service is likely to be polite but cool.

There were other problems that faced Hamilton and Lee. An information service would cost money and it was by no means certain that governing bodies would be willing to contribute. The girls' schools in particular seldom had money to spare. The girls' schools also presented another problem. It was known that they were doubtful about joining an organization that would be dominated—or so they suspected—by headmasters; and if they did join might not the closer co-operation encourage the trend they feared most—the transfer of girls to the sixth forms of boys' schools?

While it would take skilful diplomacy to bring the girls' schools in, the prep schools could be expected to demand a scheme that was at least as professional and no more expensive than the public relations effort they had been making for some thirteen years. It was also essential to the success of any scheme that the Great Schools should be seen to be involved. Much as other schools might resent Eton's pre-eminence, it was vital that Eton did not remain aloof as both it and Harrow had done during the negotiations with the Public Schools Commission. Fortunately for the future of ISIS the Fellows of Eton had just appointed Michael McCrum headmaster and he was one of the most enthusiastic and effective advocates of closer co-operation between independent schools.

In November 1970, Hamilton and Lee prompted GBA and HMC to set up a sub-committee to review the position of independent schools in the light of the Conservative election victory and in particular to consider the case for a centralized information service. The sub-committee met under Lee's chairmanship and its report *Future Policy for Public Schools* was circulated to the schools in August 1971. On the need for an information service centrally directed, the report was unequivocal:

> The independent schools have not in the past been their own best advocates. They have had little common organization and have left prospective clients to find out about them individually as and when they could. This is a weakness which should be remedied. ... Information about independent schools must, if it is to be up-to-date and reliable, be supplied by themselves and this points to the need to provide an Information Service to cover schools of all kinds. ... It would enable us to deal with press and public relations on a secure

basis of information. It would aim to reach a wider clientele than we have often served in the past. The launching of such a service would require careful preliminary study; but its inauguration is a matter of urgency.

But the problem of winning over the doubters was not so easily solved. When the sub-committee asked one of its members, Ralph Allison of Brentwood, to draft a discussion paper on an information service, his proposals were criticized by all the groups not represented on the sub-committee—the bursars, the prep schools and the girls' schools. The bursars stuck to their view that a strong central policy organization was needed before an information service. The prep schools thought Allison's proposals elegant but amateur. The girls' schools registered reservations without being very explicit on what the reservations were; the problem was, as one headmaster observed, 'the long-felt complex shared by many headmistresses that they were second-class citizens'.

It was clearly time to bring all these groups into the discussions. Suspicion of the headmasters, and a feeling of resentment that the boys' public schools should have thought that they were best fitted to organize an information service, undoubtedly added to the difficulty of bringing the independent schools together. The appointment of a Promotion Committee, under the chairmanship of Kirkpatrick Young, which included representatives of all the interested groups did something to allay suspicion and to smooth ruffled feathers, but the bursars remained unconvinced and the headmistresses played hard to get. There is a note of exasperation in Donald Wright's account of the negotiations:

> I took it upon myself to say that, despite the reservations of both the bursars and the headmistresses, neither of whom have been or were likely to be in the front line of the Independent Sector's defence compared to us headmasters, I was not prepared to go on without an Information Service and that I was quite sure I was speaking for the whole HMC.

Wright was headmaster of Shrewsbury and chairman of HMC in that year, 1971. He was not alone in experiencing impatience

75

at the attitude of bursars and headmistresses. The bursars eventually agreed not to delay the creation of the information service as long as their proposal for an effective central policy organization was acted on as soon as possible. The headmistresses proved more awkward. Like distressed gentlefolk they were at once proud and fearful of the future. They needed help but objected to what they thought was the patronizing attitude of the headmasters. In short they did not want to be taken for granted; they wanted to be won over. Headmasters, who were not strong on feminine psychology, thought the headmistresses were being obstructive for the sake of it. What assurances did the head-mistresses want?

One assurance that the headmistresses did want was that the boys' schools would at least observe the usual courtesies before admitting girls to their sixth form. HMC Committee hastened to comply. 'I am very glad to hear of HMC's action,' wrote one of the GBA negotiators, 'I think it should help a lot.' But the headmistresses were still cool about an information service. In the early months of 1972 there was a real danger that the first attempt at co-operation in the independent sector would have to go ahead without the girls' schools. No doubt some headmasters would not have been too disappointed. That the difficulties were overcome was largely due to the good sense of two people—Joyce Cadbury and Donald Lindsay. Joyce Cadbury represented the Governing Bodies of Girls' Schools Association (GBGSA) on the Promotion Committee. An ex-Chairman of Birmingham Education Committee, she had the knack of enabling disparate groups to work together. She had no illusions about headmasters or head-mistresses. 'I know that headmistresses can be very difficult,' she told Lindsay, 'but headmasters are unconsciously arrogant.' She firmly supported the concept of an information service and made it her job to win the headmistresses over. In this she had an indispensable ally in Donald Lindsay.

Lindsay had a crucial role to play in unifying the independent sector. He had just retired after a long and successful head-mastership of Malvern College. In December 1971, he was invited to spend six months organizing the proposed information service; subsequently he became its first Director. He was an inspired choice. As a former chairman of HMC he had the confidence of the boys' public schools. But what was much more important, he had the political skill and good humour needed to woo the girls' schools. He never made the mistake of talking down to headmistresses. He flattered them. They saw through it and surrendered. With Walter Hamilton, Lindsay helped to ensure that a woman—Joyce Cadbury—became the first chairman of the ISIS Joint Council, the governing body of the information service. When the national ISIS was at last formally launched, it seemed that for some years his energy, tact and resilience alone kept the ramshackle machine in the air. He was a masterly speaker, judging his audience with a precision that would have done credit to an American presidential candidate or a music-hall trooper playing the northern circuit. He handled the press more professionally than the experts and he dealt patiently with criticism of ISIS from within the independent sector. But perhaps his most important quality was his inability to take the whole business quite as seriously as some of the headmasters and headmistresses would have wished. Too stuffy for too long, hypersensitive about the risk of bad publicity and largely cut off from the mainstream of social change, many public school heads badly needed someone to persuade the rest of the world that they were human. Lindsay performed that task brilliantly. He was no less determined than they in his defence of their independence but he grasped much sooner the need to win friends. If the Promotion Committee had appointed a different retired head-master or a professional public relations man—as was suggested—the early years of ISIS would have been even more difficult.

By April 1972, Kirkpatrick Young's Promotion Committee was able to circulate the schools with a final draft of the scheme and an estimate of the cost. All independent schools recognized as efficient would be eligible to join ISIS. If all joined, the cost for each school would be small. Even so some governing bodies, still unconvinced of the value of an information service, made heavy weather of agreeing to pay.

At last in October the national ISIS was publicly launched. It was in its way as important a moment as the first gathering of the Headmasters' Conference at Uppingham in 1869. The setting for these two milestones in independent education could not have been more different. In 1869, the handful of headmasters met in 'the cruellest winter weather'; the countryside was a sodden wilderness, the school cold. In these bleak, unpromising surroundings, Thring told his guests that isolation from each other had engendered a spirit of rivalry rather than co-operation. 'Let us be rivals,' he said, 'in a hearty desire to do good work.'

ISIS was officially launched at a press conference in the Haberdashers' Hall in London. In these comfortable surroundings, Joyce Cadbury and Donald Lindsay made brief statements outlining the structure and purpose of the new organization. The regional ISIS offices would continue to provide information; the central office would handle public relations. The press asked questions; Lindsay mentioned that on the previous day he had seen the Secretary of State, Margaret Thatcher, to explain the role of ISIS. When the questions had ended drinks were served. As Lindsay chatted informally to the education correspondents, it was evident that he was already on Christian-name terms with most of them. The following day the launching of ISIS received a good press. 'Independent schools fight back', was the headline in *The Times*, and in the *Daily Telegraph*, 'United at last'. In their relations with the outside world, the independent schools had moved into the twentieth century.

The Hattersley Debate

The early days of ISIS were not easy. The public display of unity hid the fact that some schools were still sceptical of the value of a national organization, that headmistresses were now worried that the publicity material produced by ISIS would favour the boys' schools and that the bursars were still pressing for a central policy body. Donald Lindsay steered ISIS through these crosscurrents with a sensitive hand: the doubters and headmistresses were reassured, the bursars given every hope that their scheme would not be long delayed. It was a measure of his success that the opponents of independent schools were provoked into extravagant attacks. 'The public schools are on the run,' claimed the *Teachers World*, 'they have had to form ISIS, ostensibly to inform prospective parents about their schools but actually as a public relations agency to salvage some of their former awesome image. . . . The public schools have been found out. Their bluff has been called and they are straining every sinew to try to appear respectable and to present themselves as acceptable alternatives to the maintained schools.'

This was the sort of knock-about stuff that Lindsay found it easy to deal with but never used himself. Like a professional boxer sparring with a fairground gorilla, he did the minimum necessary to make his point. 'Donald Lindsay, Director of ISIS, put the case for the public schools—not assertively as of yore, but almost apologetically,' the *Teachers World* complained. Lindsay's style set the tone for the defence of independent schools for many years to come. There were backwoodsmen who wanted him to slug it out punch for punch but his approach, firm but reasonable, always prepared to see sense in his opponent's argument, never weakening his own case by protesting too much, was thoroughly vindicated in the years to come.

The potential conflicts within the independent sector caused him more headaches than the attacks of opponents. The latter might have helped him if they had been made by someone with sufficient political authority to pose a real threat to independent schools. What ISIS needed was a good war.

Roy Hattersley provided the *casus belli*. We have seen that his Cambridge speech in September 1973 expressed the new Labour policy that had been thrashed out by the National Executive's Science and Education Sub-Committee under the chairmanship of Joan Lestor. Hattersley's blunt assertion of Labour's 'serious intention' to reduce and eventually eliminate the independent sector played into ISIS's hands. ISIS had managed to obtain a copy of the speech in advance so that its response was well prepared. Lindsay rushed out two special editions of the ISIS newsletter, giving the full text of Hattersley's speech together with the overwhelmingly hostile press reaction. Hattersley had succeeded in uniting all but the left-wing press behind the principle of independence, a goal that ISIS itself might have taken many years to achieve.

The Cambridge speech also led Hattersley into a public debate on independent schools. The BBC were currently running a programme called 'Sunday Debate' in which a topical and controversial issue was argued out at length on three consecutive Sunday evenings. Hattersley agreed to take part, as did the Conservative Under-Secretary of State for Education, Norman St. John-Stevas. The producer wanted a public school head-master to take part and the choice fell on me. The reasons were that I was comparatively unknown—I had become headmaster of Westminster only three years before—and that an article I had written in *The Times* defending independent schools had caught the producer's eye. No doubt the fact that I was close at hand was an added qualification.

Hattersley's partner in the debate was the Revd Patrick Miller, a young teacher in a maintained Sixth Form College in Basingstoke. I had admired his work in the field of religious education and had recently offered him a job at Westminster. As Patrick had been enthusiastic about accepting my offer and had been frustrated only by the problem of finding accommodation in London, his advocacy of the abolition of public schools was somewhat inhibited.

The first two programmes took the form of statements by each of the four participants followed by questions and discussion under the chairmanship of Robin Day. In the final programme two assessors joined the debate to give their verdict on the arguments. The assessors chosen by the BBC were Lincoln Ralphs, the Chief Education Officer of Norfolk, and Norman Anderson, a distinguished academic lawyer.

The debate ran well for Norman St. John-Stevas and myself. Neither Hattersley nor Miller was able to make the case for abolition convincing. In the cross-questioning of our position they concentrated their fire on me but I had been well briefed by Donald Lindsay and Frank Fisher and in my opening statement had staked out a position which it was difficult to attack.

I believed then—as I believe now—that the opponents of independent schools have a good case. The schools may not create divisions in society but they help to perpetuate them; they may not deny to the state system actual resources—as Hattersley claimed—but they do deny to the state schools many of those parents who would be most likely to provide the impetus for improvement. There is a sense, therefore, in which the state schools and society as a whole would benefit from the abolition of the independent sector. But the case for allowing independent schools to exist is stronger. It is not simply that some are very good schools; to retain them for that reason would be a matter of pragmatism not principle. The question of principle involved is the freedom of individuals or groups to run efficient schools outside the provision made by the state. To remove that freedom in a democracy would be, as *The Times* argued, 'a startling trespass on individual liberty'.

In my opening statement therefore I acknowledged that the independent schools could be said to obstruct the achievement of a fairer and more harmonious society; but I argued that if the harm done by that obstruction was weighed against the claims of individual liberty there was no doubt that society would have to say that it was more important to preserve liberty than to take a short cut to equality and fraternity.

This method of defending independent schools did not please everybody. Some thought it conceded too much to the schools' opponents. But it was what I believed. It was also successful. The two assessors came down firmly on the side of the independent schools. Hattersley took his defeat with good humour but he has avoided the subject of independent schools ever since.

If I was inclined to feel pleased with my own performance I was soon brought down to earth by Westminster boys who took a sceptical view of the importance of television, by one television critic who described me as 'a perfect Jesuit inquisitor, full of silky menace', and by a correspondent who attacked the BBC for choosing as the champion of the independent schools 'the headmaster of a school in the Third Division'.

The Hattersley debate not only won support for independent schools; it also won more support for ISIS within the independent sector. Those who advocated a strong central organization to co-ordinate policy also thought that Hattersley's attack reinforced their arguments. The new Labour line had suffered a rebuff but the Party had no intention of modifying it; the independent schools had had the better of a skirmish but the war continued. If the independent schools were not to be taken by surprise again they needed more effective contacts in the political world.

Wooing Politicians

In their relations with political parties, the independent schools face a dilemma. They do not wish to be identified with a particular party, as the trade unions are with the Labour Party, yet they are bound to see the Conservatives as their natural allies in the event of any political attack. They are in the same position as a country which would prefer to be non-aligned but which depends for its defence and freedom on one of the super-powers. And like such a country, the independent schools do not wish to break off all relations with the other super-power, in this case the Labour Party.

Lindsay believed it was essential to keep a political dialogue going with Labour politicians, not all of whom would necessarily support the Hattersley line. In this he was supported by the more politically aware headmasters such as Frank Fisher and by influential governors such as Sir William Hayter of Winchester who had been convinced by Hugh Gaitskell that the abolitionists were a minority in the Labour Party. But it was a delicate area because Labour M.P.s were not keen to have it publicized that they had met—however informally—representatives of inde-pendent schools. At the same time there were those within the independent sector who would have regarded such a meeting as only comparable with a discussion between a British government and the IRA.

Meetings with Labour politicians were, therefore, small scale, informal and unpublicized; and whenever possible they were arranged as joint meetings with Labour and Conservative M.P.s so that the emphasis could be on an exchange of views rather than on political lobbying. From these discreet contacts, the independent schools formed the impression that not all Labour M.P.s supported the Hattersley line but that such M.P.s as did not were a minority in the Party, not a majority as Gaitskell had suggested. The Labour M.P.s did, however, strongly criticize the schools' failure to project a more favourable image, and declared themselves willing to visit the schools to see for themselves. They urged the schools to do all that they could to make the case for independence known to the moderate Labour M.P.s. Fred Willey, the M.P. for Sunderland North and a future vice-chairman of the Parliamentary Labour Party, offered to act as a liaison between the schools and those Labour M.P.s who were not ill-disposed.

The fruits of this initiative were disappointing. The idea of an informal liaison between the schools and the Labour Party quickly disappeared when Willey discovered that he was too busy to undertake the task. When it came to the point even those Labour M.P.s who opposed abolition—and these included a future Secretary of State, Reg Prentice—were reluctant to be seen to be helping the independent sector. After this the informal contacts became few and far between though both Donald Lindsay and his successor as Director of ISIS, Tim Devlin, made a point of keeping in touch with Labour education spokesmen. By the end of the seventies, the independent schools, while not abandoning the concept of a dialogue with Labour, had become more sceptical about the chances of winning over even the right wing of the Party.

Though the Liberal Party wielded little political influence it was worth cultivating. There was no danger of Liberals advocating abolition but it was important to discover how strong their support for independence was and in particular where they stood on the direct grant and charitable status. As a member of the Liberal Party, I was able to provide a link between the Party and the independent schools. In October 1972, the Chairman of the Liberal Party, Richard Wainwright, met Frank Fisher, Donald

Wright and myself at Westminster. Once again the political contact proved a disappointment. Wainwright had not done his homework. I noted in my diary for that day; 'The Chairman of the Party obviously knows little of the complex issues involved; he keeps saying what the Young Liberals think as though he was conscious of them looking over his shoulder.'

Wainwright did reaffirm Liberal opposition to any proposals to abolish independent schools or to make fee-paying illegal. On the question of the direct grant and charitable status it was clear that the Liberals had not thought out their position. Although I served on the Party's Education Panel, I found it difficult to discover what Liberal education policy was. Liberal M.P.s had the same problem. When the direct grant schools were being debated in the Commons, a Liberal M.P. who intended to speak telephoned me: 'Tell me, John, are we in favour or against the direct grant?'

This political amateurism made Liberals uncertain allies; in the event they were not prepared to oppose the ending of the direct grant and would have supported Labour over the removal of charitable status if that issue had come before the House.

If the Labour and Liberal politicians presented an elusive target to the independent schools' political initiatives, the Conservatives presented an even more complex problem and in some ways a greater disappointment. There has always been an element of ambivalence in relationships between the Conservative Party and the independent schools. Though Conservatives are unequivocally in favour of a mixed economy in education, they are sensitive to the accusation that, with 80 per cent of its M.P.s coming from independent schools, the Party is merely defending privilege and is not interested in the maintained schools. So the Conservatives are as anxious as the independent schools that the association between the two should not be too close in the popular mind. That does not prevent Conservative M.P.s sending their sons and daughters to independent schools usually as a matter of course. Like respectable Victorian gentlemen in their relationship with ladies of easy virtue, some Tories do not object to using the schools in private but do not want to be seen with them in public. They are, however, much less blatantly inconsistent than those Labour politicians who rage against privilege in education yet pay fees for their children to attend independent schools.

The relationshp is further complicated by the existence on both sides of people who believe that the independent schools should be more closely associated with the state system and who blame the other side for not being more constructive on this issue. When Alan Barker criticized the 'Conservative failure to give any help in making the public schools of more use to the community as a whole,' he was reflecting a fairly widespread view among headmasters that the Tories had missed an opportunity in the 1950s of working out an acceptable form of integration. But the attitude of the Conservative Party was one of live and let live; it would not stand by and see the independent schools abolished but neither would it yield to demands that the schools' position should be made more favourable, particularly in the field of taxation. The independent schools divide the Conservative Party just as they do Labour; and Conservative policy, which may seem negative to the heads of independent schools, represents a compromise between the conflicting views. Angus Maude has described the divisions with the Party on this issue:

> The Conservative right wing, backed probably by the majority of active supporters in the constituencies, is for upholding the independent schools at all costs, including tax rebates for fees. But some Conservative politicians are genuinely worried about the 'dual system' of education, regarding it as an increasingly anachronistic and divisive element in our society. . . . Tory social reformers, imbued with the Disraelian idea of an unfragmented society, are inevitably worried by the divisive effects of the 'dual system'.

As Maude points out, 'the dichotomy between these two sets of views could scarcely be more complete.' It is a dichotomy that the independent schools have been slow to recognize and its existence continues to inhibit a more creative approach by the Party to the problem of the independent schools.

The complexities and disappointments have not deterred the independent schools from continuing to seek a dialogue with politicians of all persuasions. 'Cultivate friends everywhere,' was Donald Lindsay's advice, 'they will be needed.' What such cultivation has achieved cannot be measured with any precision but the political initiatives have at least ensured that politicians are much better informed about the arguments for an independent sector than they were fifteen years ago.

The Independent Schools Joint Committee

From the start, the approaches to politicians underlined the need to have a single body that could represent all independent schools. ISIS could put the case for independence and provide an information service for prospective parents, but it had not been designed to decide matters of policy nor did it have the authority to do so.

The creation in 1974 of the Independent Schools Joint Committee (ISJC)—as the new policy body was to be called—caused fewer difficulties than had been envisaged when the bursars first put forward the idea. The two successful years of ISIS's operation made the next step towards unity appear both easy and logical. There were some misgivings, however. Members of HMC feared they would 'speak with a much less powerful voice than we do now,' if HMC was forced to submerge its identity in a much larger organization. Some headmasters were reluctant to be tied to the girls' schools which they regarded as a liability rather than an additional strength. One senior headmaster put it bluntly in a memorandum on the bursars' original proposal: 'I do not believe myself that we should be wise to associate our fortunes with the girls' schools. It would seem to me that we must continue to seek our own salvation in future.'

Fortunately for the independent sector, the chairman of HMC in 1974 was Michael McCrum, who was convinced of the need for a central policy body and who had the authority to reassure his colleagues that HMC's freedom of action would not be curtailed or its salvation risked by joining a convoy of less powerful vessels.

As had been the case with ISIS, ISJC's successful birth owed much to a few individuals. The invitation to Lord Belstead to be the first chairman provided the Committee with leadership of high quality. John Belstead, a young Conservative peer, had until the previous year been Under-Secretary of State for Education in Heath's Government. He knew his way round the Department of Education and Science and, unlike some of his colleagues on the Committee, he knew precisely what was and was not politically possible. He was an excellent chairman, above the polite infighting among the different groups but sensitive to the conflict of interests.

Belstead was assisted by a most able Secretary to the Committee in Jack Walesby, the bursar of Bedales. It fell to Walesby to provide that service that the bursars had always wanted: an efficient exchange of information and expertise on practical issues, from fire precautions to capital transfer tax. At this level ISJC was immediately successful. On matters of policy ISJC had to move more cautiously. A committee that had to include representatives of every interest in the independent sector was an unwieldy and unsuitable forum for the detailed discussion of policy, so a small advisory committee, under Desmond Lee, was established; it was in this advisory committee that a common policy on a number of potentially divisive issues was forged.

ISJC could not and did not wish to dictate to individual schools how they should run their affairs. It could and did provide an arena in which conflicts, such as that between headmasters and headmistresses over the transfer of girls to boys' sixth forms, could be discussed, if not always finally resolved. It was also able to respond to challenges that affected independent schools as a whole: in November 1974 it gave evidence on behalf of all independent schools to the Goodman Committee on the law relating to charities, and in 1977 it negotiated with the Department of Education and Science on Labour's decision to discontinue the status of 'recognition as efficient' for independent schools. In the latter case there was a real but not immediately obvious threat to independent schools: if the schools were not formally recognized as efficient, their teachers would not qualify for membership of the State Teachers' Superannuation Scheme. If governing bodies had had to provide pensions at comparable rates, there would have been a swingeing increase in fees and some of the smaller schools may well have disappeared. ISJC spotted this danger and carried sufficient weight to obtain from the Secretary of State an assurance that teachers in independent schools would not be excluded from the State Teachers' Scheme.

These and other unglamorous but important achievements fully justified the existence of ISJC. Where it was less successful was in marshalling the forces of the independent sector in defence of the direct grant schools. When in 1975, the Labour Government made clear its intention to phase out the direct grant, ISIS ran an energetic campaign to rally public opinion against the move. But neither ISIS nor ISJC could disguise the division that existed between the fully independent schools and those that received the direct grant. It is impossible to make sense of public school politics in this period unless the nature of this division is understood.

The origin of the division lay in the fact that the fully independent schools tended to be boarding rather than day; they also tended to be richer, more fashionable and more firmly linked to the influential classes. Their direct grant colleagues were the poor relations. When some of the direct grant schools achieved better results in examinations, the fully independent schools were inclined to dismiss that sort of education as 'narrow' and to lay stress on the education of the all-round man that their schools provided. The division was partly one of tradition and style and partly one of class and wealth. The relations between the two types of school were too often informed by snobbery on one side and suspicion on the other.

The headmasters of the fully independent schools were usually ignorant of how the direct grant system worked and had little feel for the aims and atmosphere of a direct grant school. In the Headmasters' Conference it was rare for a direct grant headmaster to reach the top; in the thirty-five years since the war only four headmasters of direct grant schools were chairmen of the Conference, even though the direct grant schools provided a third of the membership. Representation on the committee also compared unfavourably with that of the fully independent schools and particularly with the representation of the Great Schools. Two-thirds of Conference chairmen since the war came from the Great Schools; Eton, Winchester, Westminster, Rugby and Shrewsbury were the only schools to provide two chairmen in this period. In the exclusive dining clubs for HMC head-masters—The Twenty-Seven and The Gang—direct grant schools were even more thinly represented.

One result of this division was that the fully independent schools did not give wholehearted support to the campaign to save the direct grant schools. There was also an element of self-interest in their attitude. With fees rising steeply, the heads both feared and resented the competition from direct grant schools whose fees were being kept artificially low. It must have seemed to some headmasters of fully independent schools that the sooner the direct grant went the better. ISIS warned that failure to protest at the withdrawal of the direct grant would encourage the Labour Government to attack the whole independent sector, but the fully independent schools remained lukewarm in their support for the campaign.

In the independent sector's failure to save the direct grant, and in particular in the ambivalent attitude of the fully independent schools, lay the seeds of an even more divisive issue—the Assisted Places Scheme—which is discussed in Chapter 8.

The final years of the 1974–9 Labour Government found the independent schools in confident mood despite the loss of the direct grant and the continued threat of the removal of charitable status. ISIS and ISJC were well established. In 1977 Tim Devlin succeeded Donald Lindsay as Director of ISIS. Devlin, a professional journalist and former education correspondent on *The Times*, brought different experience and expertise to the role but like Lindsay he believed that the opponents of independent schools were best won over by argument not abuse. He encouraged the schools to be more open to the media, whether it was over the publication of exam results or co-operation with television producers. He took the view that at a time when dissatisfaction with maintained schools was widespread there was much to be gained by allowing the public to see what actually happened in independent schools. As a result two boys' public schools, Westminster and Radley, became the subject of BBC documentaries. When the Westminster film was shown in September 1979, it had an audience of 12 million. Though some of the school's old boys were disconcerted to find that the school had changed since their day, the press reactions seemed to confirm Devlin's confidence. The *Daily Telegraph*'s opinion that the film was the best public relations for public schools since the Battle of Waterloo may have been putting it rather high but there was little doubt that the independent schools' greater openness to the media was paying off.

When the Conservatives won the election in 1979, the new Chairman of ISIS, Dorothy Dakin, wrote in the ISIS Newsletter: 'Politics are fickle; the years ahead are uncertain. We must have a strong unassailable place in the British education system, before the Left threatens us again. We have a chance, let us make the most of it.'

The past fifteen years of increasingly unified and expert response to political challenge had already given the independent schools a strong position. Whether that position could be made unassailable remained to be seen.

5

The Challenge of Educational and Social Change in the Sixties

The threat of political action by the Labour Party was a less immediate problem for the heads of independent schools than the educational ferment of the sixties and what appeared to be the threat of mutiny among their own pupils. The years of political challenge and response coincided with a period of extraordinary restlessness and change in independent schools, the importance of which it is still difficult to assess. The picture is complicated by the simultaneous easing of restrictions and tightening of academic organization.

No one doubts that the schools underwent a variety of internal changes in the years 1964–79. What is in doubt is how profound and lasting the changes were. There are some who talk of the 'public school revolution', which radically altered the priorities and lifestyle in the schools. Others see the changes of these years as evolutionary, an acceleration of the process perhaps but not a radical break with the past. A complementary view is held by those who believe that the essential modernization of the independent schools was carried out in the decade before 1964 by men returning from the war and bringing with them a wider experience and an impatience with the stuffier aspects of tradition. Finally, there are those who deny that any fundamental change has occurred and who accuse the independent schools of skilful window-dressing in the face of public criticism.

We are too close to the events to place them in their historical perspective. In a hundred years' time the changes may be seen as interesting but not particularly important adaptations to social and educational pressures; it seems equally possible that they may come to be regarded as the most fundamental reforms in independent schools since those initiated by Dr Arnold and his disciples. In the period we are concerned with there was no Dr Arnold, no single figure who stamped the reforms with his own ideals; it was a characteristic of the changes that they were not inspired by a coherent educational philosophy; the independent schools stumbled into the future, knocking over a number of sacred cows in the process but with no clear idea of where they were going. If a revolution occurred it was pragmatic, not part of a grand design.

It is difficult now to recapture the sense of optimism and excitement that greeted Harold Wilson's election victory in 1964. Men and women who would never have identified themselves as Labour supporters nevertheless felt that a new era was beginning. What no one had bargained for was that Wilson's period of office would coincide with a social upheaval that had little to do with Labour policies. The chief characteristic of this upheaval was an attack on authority in all its forms. The authority of the law, of government, of the church, of parents, of conventional morality and of social status, was satirized, defied, challenged at every point. Restraint and restriction were anathema. William Blake's 'Damn braces: bless relaxes', was the theme. The activities and antics of the young, particularly of university students, caught the eye but in fact the permissive or self-indulgent society had been created by adults to suit themselves; they had not appreciated that the young would seize the opportunity to assert their own independence and would push the limits of individual choice and freedom further back than the adults had ever intended.

It was a confusing time, at once exciting and sour. There was a whiff of decadence about Britain in those years but it was also a time of idealism. Teenagers and students in particular were caught up in what appeared to be a movement for a better world. They experienced the rare joy of a sense of purpose; and of unity too, for the pop culture seemed to eradicate the barriers of class and nationality. The pop culture had the additional advantage of excluding the adult generation; with its own saints and martyrs, its own language and customs, it was a haven, a secure base to which the young could escape from what they saw as the hypocrisies and shabby compromises of the adult world and from which they could sally forth to the attack. The arrival of a younger generation with money and with their own culture exacerbated the inevitable failures of communication and understanding between the generations. The new permissiveness gave the young an opportunity for self-expression in dress and manners; drugs gave them a means of shocking their parents while indulging in the adolescent search for new experience; the Vietnam War gave them a cause.

The adults responded to the youthful challenge in a variety of ways but the dominant emotion seems to have been fear. Parents were afraid of their children, teachers of their pupils. Fear led some adults to over-react, interpreting any youthful peccadillo as the first shot in a revolutionary war. It led others to go over to the enemy, or to use a more appropriate metaphor, to go native; they tried to identify with the young and usually made fools of themselves. One distinguished anthropologist announced that parents had more to learn from their children than vice versa. Some adults lost their nerve altogether: most did not. For any adult with direct responsibility for the young it was a difficult, even unhappy period.

There was no way in which independent schools could avoid being hit by this social upheaval. As institutions identified with the establishment and exercising authority over the young, they were both the object of attack and the theatre of conflict. They were not disrupted as were many of the universities. The open rebellions that had occurred in the older public schools at the end of the eighteenth century were not repeated. But there was guerrilla warfare in the form of protest against the traditional compulsions they imposed. Preparatory schools dealing with the younger age group were not as much affected as secondary schools, few of which escaped the troubles. Boys' schools were more turbulent than girls', boarding schools more so than day schools. If this chapter concentrates on the boys' public schools, it is because they bore the brunt of the unrest.

The historian in me would like to identify the starting point of the guerrilla war: the first occasion on which all the boys stood in silence while the organist played the hymn or marched off parade to the astonishment of their commanding officer. But if there is a Tennis Court Oath or a Storming of the Bastille in this story, I have not found it. Slowly, unevenly, disaffection spread through the public schools during the latter half of the sixties. It reached a climax in most schools in 1969, often referred to now by headmasters as the most difficult years of their careers.

The impact of the wave of unrest varied from school to school. In some schools the old compulsions went down like ninepins: attendance at chapel, wearing school uniform, playing the prescribed major sport, joining the Combined Cadet Force—all became more or less optional. In most schools, however, the authorities yielded slowly, sometimes clumsily, so that old compulsions were modified rather than abolished. A few schools managed to retain the old compulsory system intact during these years and were in a position to introduce changes in their own time during the less hectic seventies.

Those of us who became headmasters in the mid-sixties and who had to steer schools through the cross-currents of the ensuing years are inclined to picture the school we inherited as a bleak, unreformed institution, ripe for change. There were schools that had changed little in style, curriculum and physical environment since the pre-war years but they were few and far between. In most schools the changes of the late sixties that seemed so radical at the time were made possible by the changes that had already been made in the fifties.

The key to the post-war modernization of the public schools was the breaking of the incestuous career pattern of the pre-war masters: from public school to Oxford or Cambridge and back again to public school to teach. In many cases they went back to their own schools. The great majority of the men teaching in public schools between the wars had themselves been educated at public school and Oxbridge. Their experience of the world was narrow: in many cases the only years they had spent outside the closed world of a boarding school were those at Oxford or

Cambridge, universities that were then dominated by public school men and the public school ethos. As schoolmasters some of these men were not surprisingly little more than overgrown schoolboys. Frank Fisher, who went to Repton from the Army in 1947 recalls that the pre-war masters still on the staff 'accepted the customs and habits and limitations of the public schools as being both desirable and immutable; they brought with them no new ideas and were little concerned with the practice of philosophy of education outside their own campus.'

The war did not change the high proportion of masters educated at public school and the ancient universities; Graham Kalton's 1966 survey found that in the independent boarding schools 73 per cent of the masters had been educated at public school and 83 per cent at Oxford or Cambridge. But the war had forced men out into a different world, sometimes for as long as seven years. When Frank Fisher joined the Repton staff, eighteen returned soldiers joined in the next two years.

> We were superimposed upon a group of ineffective wartime appointments and residue of pre-war men, all of whom retained both the attitudes and the lifestyle of the thirties. Our contribution was dramatic. We swept away many of the old-fashioned attitudes that we found unattractive, such as power in the hands of the senior boys, the cloistered and introverted life of the school, the sheer squalor of much of the accommodation, the old-fashioned and inefficient arrangements.

In the 1950s, when these men with war experience became headmasters, the momentum of change was stepped up. In 1954 Frank Fisher was appointed Warden of St. Edward's School, Oxford; his predecessor had been appointed in 1925. Fisher set about the task of modernization with characteristic energy:

> It fell to me to abolish personal fagging, eliminate boy beating, arrange for hot rather than cold water in the showers, alter the dress, make chapel services more relevant, increase the activities: Duke of Edinburgh scheme, camping, trips overseas, craft work, art and pottery, music for the many, endless societies, more minor games and so on. More important was

the process of trying to make the community of a school civilized, both so far as personal relationships were concerned and so far as physical comfort was concerned. In all this we were helped most by the returned warriors and later by those who had at least some experience away from school on National Service.

A similar process of modernization was occurring in other schools that appointed new headmasters with wartime experience during the fifties. But this period of modernization had its limits: pre-war headmasters and assistant masters could not be bulldozed into accepting all the reforms the new men wanted and there was seldom enough money to modernize the plant. Most important, the tight framework of compulsion that controlled the lives of the boys remained largely unchanged. In the early sixties it was still the norm that a boy had to attend chapel every day and twice on Sunday; play the major sport whether he liked it or not; join the Combined Cadet Force; and wear a school uniform, every item of which was prescribed in the school rules. He was probably compelled to attend the school play and the school concert. His movements were strictly controlled by bounds and bells. Fagging and corporal punishment were common practice; in many schools the prefects had the power to beat other boys. A hierarchy of prefects or monitors kept the machinery of compulsion running and in return enjoyed privileges that allowed them to escape the more disagreeable aspects of the machine themselves. For all pupils, whatever their position in the hierarchy, the secret of success—and survival—was to conform.

It was this system of compulsion and hierarchy that provoked the greatest hostility when the 'teenage revolution' reached the public school. Such a system could not co-exist for long with the new wave of permissiveness in personal behaviour and increasing emphasis on individuality and non-conformity.

The demand that the individual should be allowed to 'do his own thing' was very soon in conflict with the school's insistence on certain standards of dress and appearance. The *casus belli* was the length of boys' hair. To the young, short hair was identified with the adult world, with the military and the police, with 'squareness'. To grow your hair long was to identify with other young people in their rebellion against convention. It was also seen, paradoxically, as a gesture of individuality. Long hair had other overtones: it was cavalier rather than roundhead; it suggested artiness as distinct from heartiness; in some ways that was not very clear to adults, it was an expression of adolescent sexuality.

Headmasters and parents found themselves fighting a battle they had not chosen; they thought that it was their duty to resist the growth but they were not sure why. A few headmasters chose to ignore the phenomenon; they appealed to history and pointed out to irate governors and old boys that the length of hair was just a question of fashion. The governors and old boys thought this a cover for loss of nerve and may well have been right. The majority of headmasters grasped the nettle, not because they had particularly strong views about long hair but because they did not wish to be regarded as weak. Weakness is a label that only the strongest headmasters can afford to wear. Elaborate instructions were issued, often after lengthy discussion with senior staff, defining as precisely as possible the point at which the growing hair broke the school rules: 'the hair must not cover the ears or touch the collar' was a favourite formula. Though laughable in retrospect, it was serious enough at the time. By issuing these regulations, even the most politically sophisticated headmasters provoked dumb insolence—their less astute colleagues had to face organized protests.

A similar battle was fought over school uniform which was seen both as an instrument for imposing conformity and as a badge of élitism that distinguished the public school boy from his contemporaries. The desire to be identified with other young people regardless of class was a common if not very deeply rooted emotion in the affluent sixties; it disappeared when times got hard, inflation and unemployment driving the young back into their class laagers. But while it lasted, the classlessness added a not unattractive idealistic flavour to the youth culture. Public school boys affected an accent that was, if not quite working class, sufficiently broad to dissociate them from school and parental background. Some still do but now it has more to do with football than the belief in a classless society.

The egalitarian thrust in the teenage revolution led a few boys to renounce the advantages of a privileged education; they left their public school and went to the local maintained school. Their headmasters sometimes dismissed them as drop-outs, as though anyone who would exchange a public school education for a comprehensive one must have lost the will to live. There were drop-outs from the public schools in the sixties who drifted off into this or that hippie limbo and usually took many years to find their way back into the mainstream of society. But they were distinct from the boys who made a conscious decision to reject what they regarded as privilege.

Egalitarianism also prompted some boys to join the attack on competition: marks, places and prizes were seen as inimical to the idea of a free and caring society; they set boy against boy and encouraged the unattractive habits of the adult rat-race.

The majority of rebellious or just restless teenagers in public schools did not bother much with such philosophical concepts as equality and privilege. They may have aired their views on the evils of authority and the benefits of freedom but their goals were strictly practical ones: less compulsory chapel, more opportunity to get out of the school to smoke, drink and meet girls, fewer duties, lighter punishments. They resented the machinery of restriction and compulsion because it was more and more out of step with the freedom and comfort they enjoyed at home. In a very English way, they had no theories—they just wanted results.

The demands for greater freedom led boys to defy the school rules. The fashion for the use of psychedelic drugs led them to break the law of the land. The drug culture presented the school authorities with their most serious challenge. Few, if any, public schools were entirely free of the problem, which was exacerbated by the authorities' ignorance of the subject and by their unwillingness to discuss it. At meetings of headmasters in the late sixties almost any subject was discussed other than the pupils' use of drugs; no one wanted to admit in public that his school was affected. Some headmasters pretended that the problem did not exist. Those who did follow up the rumours and who punished offenders, usually by expulsion, not infrequently found that the case was reported in the national press. Ironically it was the schools that took some action that tended to acquire the unenviable reputation of having a drug problem. Headmasters of country boarding schools assured parents that this was a problem of the schools in the cities but those of us who have headmastered in both know that this was not true. Cannabis in particular found its way into the most remote rural establishments.

It is not easy to assess how widespread the problem was in independent schools. The drug culture was secretive and difficult to penetrate. There was more rumour and gossip than hard fact. Illegal drugs were a symbol of rebellion as much as a means of exploring new experience. The secret world with its own slang provided another method of excluding adults. Attempts by headmasters to educate their pupils about the legal and physiological effects of using these drugs were rare for the same reason that headmasters were reluctant to talk about the question; if they lectured on the dangers it might be taken to imply that there was a problem. In practice, the young probably knew more about the subject, including the dangers, than the adults. Headmasters and housemasters, though not so naïve as their boys believed, found it hard to keep up with the swiftly changing argot of the drug culture.

Of all the problems that divided the generations in independent schools in this period, the one that most challenged the school authorities to search their own hearts and examine their own position, was that of compulsory attendance at religious worship. It was one of the most important too because most of the schools had explicitly Christian foundations. School prospectuses usually emphasized this point. The Cheltenham College prospectus of the time read: 'Chapel is intended to be central in the school in more than its geographical position and the School Day begins there with a short service of worship which all boys attend.' The concept of the chapel as the heart of the school was the theme of the headmaster of Christ's Hospital's address to the Headmasters' Conference in 1972. Dr David Newsome asked his audience to imagine that their school had been destroyed by some appalling catastrophe and that they were called upon to rebuild it from scratch. The building goes ahead but something is wrong:

> Both the new headmaster and the chaplain, who as boys many years ago had dim recollections of what the school had been like, knew that when this work had been done and the school was operational again it looked not unlike the original. But . . . something was missing. Lessons were in progress, school matches were being played again—but the community was lifeless. Its heart refused to beat. And then the answer came: they had left until last the rebuilding of the chapel, which was still just a heap of rubble at the side of the quad. Because this had not come first, the heart could not beat, and their previous efforts had been in vain.

Dr Newsome was a distinguished historian of Victorian society and for his audience his parable had a distinctly Victorian, even archaic ring. Had the chapel ever been the heart of the school or had that been the initial intention but ultimate delusion of the great Victorian headmasters? The headmasters of the sixties and seventies often used the Christian foundation argument as a means of discrediting Labour plans to take over their schools. Religious freedom is a powerful rallying cry in a country that does not take its religion too seriously. But the headmasters were honest enough to admit that they could not altogether share Dr Newsome's vision. There was no doubt that chapel services had influenced generations of public schoolboys but not perhaps in the way that headmasters such as Newsome imagined. Chapel was part of the routine, like lessons, games and field days; and as part of the routine it became an element in the grown man's nostalgia for boyhood. It was not so much Christian truth that he took away from all those compulsory services but a longing for atmosphere, for the faces of young friends, for the familiar hymns, above all for a sense of belonging.

In the Summer 1964 issue of *The Marlburian*, Ulric Nisbet

recalls a pre-1914 Marlborough and describes his visits to the school as an old boy:

> I never return to Marlborough without visiting the Chapel. Especially do I like the evening service when the serene beauty of the interior and the faces of the boys—seemingly identical with those of my generation—mingle in harmony with the slow chanting of the *Nunc Dimittis* and with the nostalgic evocations of the hymn. Far-strayed from orthodoxy, nevertheless I find something unspoilt and timeless in that orthodox atmosphere, very well worth taking with me into the turmoil of the world.

By the mid-sixties the contradictions underlying the practice of compulsory chapel were dangerously close to the surface. Boys sensed that this was the weakest part of the engine of compulsion. The chapel service, which in many schools had the flavour of an army church parade, had been accepted without much questioning by previous generations, but now the tide of Christian observance in society had gone far out. Few boys attended church in the holidays. The contrast between an increasingly secular society and the attempt to maintain the tradition of the Christian school, made chapel services vulnerable to the charges of hypocrisy and indoctrination. The services themselves were too often mechanical and unimaginative. It seemed to the boys that the occasion was used to reinforce the hierarchy rather than to demonstrate the Christian nature of the school community. The seating arrangements were designed both to emphasize the individual's point in the structure of authority and to ensure good discipline. The headmaster's stall was aloof; housemasters and prefects were strategically positioned to note those who failed to sing or nodded off. Masters' wives and matrons sat in a place apart known to the boys as the 'hen pen'. If parents came they sat in the back or in the gallery.

In practice these arrangements were the best way of marshalling a large congregation and checking absentees but rebellious boys could be forgiven for giving them a less favourable interpretation. Good chaplains made sense of the occasion despite the difficulties. Bad ones floundered. What had in the past been accepted as part of the routine was now seen by some boys as a hollow sham. Chapel was also an ideal situation in which to challenge authority. By refusing to sing and bow their heads in prayer, boys could reduce the service to an embarrassing farce. School authorities, and particularly headmasters, are at their most vulnerable on formal public occasions. If they do nothing in the face of open defiance they may be deemed cowardly; if they lose their cool they appear foolish; if they tell the boys to sing and are met with further silence, their position is undermined. When the whole school community and visitors are present, the headmaster has little room for manoeuvre. Divine service in particular does not lend itself to dramatic interventions by authority.

During these years there were few headmasters who did not have to face some sort of protest in chapel. Most had the sense neither to ignore the protest nor to attempt to tackle it head on in the middle of the service. There were ways of dealing with these things, though it was not always easy to think of the right solution at the time. The most effective formula was this.

At the end of the service, the headmaster asked the visitors and the staff to leave. Alone with the school, he told them that he recognized that some of them had grievances, but that a mass protest in the presence of visitors was not the way to go about things. He avoided peevishness and sarcasm, the two qualities that would immediately alienate a schoolboy audience. He made no promises or threats. By removing the staff and speaking to the boys on his own he had in one simple gesture abolished the oppressive sense of hierarchy. They were his boys and he was their headmaster; if they could not work things out together then they had come to a pretty pass. With just the right touch of humour he suggested that further protests would hardly be necessary. If he spoke well he won over the majority of the school, who would be only too pleased to get back to normal next Sunday. The disaffected minority he had little chance of winning over but the important thing was to alienate them from their unpoliticized contemporaries. With any luck the next chapel service went tolerably well.

Headmasters who survived these interesting diversions with their reputation intact may not always have appreciated that such public protests were a recurring theme in the history of public schools. What was more, the passive protests of the sixties were very tame compared to those of the past. Even that great flogger, Dr Keate, headmaster of Eton at the beginning of the nineteenth century, was shouted down in the College chapel, while a few years earlier the headmaster of Winchester had had to call in the militia to dislodge rebellious boys at the point of a bayonet.

Behind the rebellions of the eighteenth century was the boys' resentment at changes that would curtail their traditional privileges. Behind the chapel protests of the sixties was a deeper malaise. The concept of the Christian community, so central to the tradition of most of these schools, seemed increasingly difficult to square, not only with the secularization of society but also with the quality of relationships that the traditional hierarchy imposed. One headmaster, Derek Seymour of Bloxham, initiated liberal reforms at this time precisely because he did not believe that the relationships dictated by the rigid structure of the traditional public school were consistent with the Christian gospel the school had been founded to teach. In doing so he not only transformed relationships in the school, but paved the way for the Bloxham Project which is discussed at the end of Chapter 6.

It was, then, on relationships rather than on rules and restrictions that the teenage revolution put the greatest pressure. Overnight—or so it appeared—schools went sour. Experienced masters who thought they understood boys found that they could make no contact with them. Housemasters in particular, who bore the brunt of the youthful resentment of authority, could no longer rely on the expected response from boys of any age. Younger masters sometimes sympathized with the boys' demands and in a few cases aided and abetted them in their protests. Relationships between masters and boys, between masters and colleagues, and between the masters and the headmaster were put under strain. Once the clear structure of the hierarchy began to break, relations between individuals in the school could no longer be dictated by status. It was at this point that the concept of a Christian community was most seriously challenged and in almost all cases it was found wanting. What had been thought to be a Christian community turned out to be only a community whose structure relieved individuals of the necessity of having to work out their relations with one another. Without the support of their place in the hierarchy, masters would not know how to relate to boys.

What appears to have happened in the late sixties is that the pupils' questioning of authority exposed the adults' unresolved adolescence. That is to say the teachers—in common with other adults—retained from their own adolescence uncertainty about identity and an unresolved ambivalence about their own worth as individuals. In the unquestioning atmosphere of the old-style public school these uncertainties and ambivalence could remain hidden. Routine, status, hierarchy provided security and an anaesthetic against the pain of self-questioning. It is not surprising therefore that in the late sixties the heads and staffs of public schools found themselves confused, even frightened, by the attack on the existing structure of authority and relationships.

Whether this is a convincing psychological explanation I am not sure. Masters are bound to feel insecure if the whole basis of authority and discipline is challenged. There is, after all, an element of bluff in the control of 600 adolescent boys by fifty masters; if the 600 take it into their heads to mutiny, it requires a steady nerve and remarkably quick thinking to restore authority. During the eighteenth-century public school rebellions, a Westminster boy, Francis Burdett, led an uprising against the headmaster, Dr Smith. In front of the whole school, Burdett stepped forward to present his revolutionary demands. Dr Smith struck him on the head with a club. When Burdett recovered he was promptly expelled. The mutiny subsided as suddenly as it had arisen.

Such vigorous methods would certainly have crossed the minds of Dr Smith's twentieth-century counterparts, but it was wishful thinking. Rebellious boys were expelled, but not many.

None was hit on the head, though no doubt some deserved to be. Headmasters were reluctant to expel rebels; they were afraid of stirring up more trouble and they were inhibited by at least some sympathy with what the rebellious boys were trying to achieve. Some headmasters even played the dangerous game of using the rebels to put pressure on reactionary housemasters to accept reforms.

Fear of the boys was a potent factor. It could no more be admitted than a handful of British soldiers controlling a remote imperial outpost could admit they were afraid of the natives. But the underlying fear accounted for some of the more confused and panicky responses to the first stirrings of unrest. And yet, despite the organized protests and the awkward, even ugly moments, there is little evidence that the *majority* of boys positively wanted changes to occur. In the Autumn 1968 issue of *The Tauntonian*, a questionnaire of pupils' attitudes revealed that the majority were in favour of compulsory sport and chapel, and the retention of corporal punishment; two-thirds thought that relations between boys and staff were good or satisfactory. It is probably true that in most schools changes occurred as a result of an interaction between the school authorities—usually the headmaster—and a minority of pupils who were prepared to use in a somewhat modified form the tactics of the militants in the universities. The majority of boys and masters were not actively involved; the dominant feeling was probably one of impatience that the headmaster would not make up his mind which changes he was going to permit. Boys in particular are very quick to adapt to what seems to be the new *status quo*. What neither they nor the staff like is a sense of drift: and during the late sixties, schools did appear to be drifting without a clear policy or goal. The problem for the headmasters was not simply what changes or concessions to greater freedom they should make; the more fundamental question was on what educational idea or philosophy the changes were to be based. The deeper malaise that the militant boys were consciously aware of or sensed intuitively was that headmasters lacked a coherent educational philosophy; they were seen as men who were good managers, public relations experts and fund raisers but not as men who knew what they were doing and why. No doubt that was a harsh judgement on most headmasters but there was an element of truth in it; and the feeling that the man at the helm was not sure where he was going allowed disaffection to spread.

Before looking at the changes that were made as a result of the restless sixties, it might be helpful to consider two personal comments on the mood of the time, one from inside the system and one from outside.

John Morris arrived at Sedbergh School as a young master straight from university in 1969. He had been educated at the school himself and remembered clearly the mood of the community before the troubles. Sedbergh, in Cumbria, is a sixteenth-century foundation famous for combining excellence in rugby football with excellence in the arts, notably music. It is remote from the cities and from the affluent South where the discontent of pupils and students was thought to be at its worst. Morris describes the Sedbergh he found in 1969:

> In 1969 I still had some very vivid impressions of my own schooldays as a boy at Sedbergh in the early sixties when, surrounded by a number of very gifted academics, games-players and thoroughly enthusiastic adolescents, I had thought the School a marvellous place. I had enjoyed the active life and the prefectorial responsibility which at that time seemed to be flourishing. On my return in the winter of 1969 I found a very different atmosphere. The dissatisfaction with the restrictions and traditions imposed upon the VIth formers, coupled with the challenge to authority which was being made at that time, manifested itself at Sedbergh in a number of ways, the anti-team games feeling being just one. Rugby football, for years one of the great features of Sedbergh life, was seriously under pressure. It was no coincidence that the school XVs of those years were not of the usual standard. I can remember rather dreading the prospect of having to referee an inter-house rugger match. It was a major problem to keep the players actually participating seriously. The ball would be kicked into touch and a suitably long period of time would elapse before anyone would trouble to fetch it. This apathy was

not entirely confined to games. Support for music and drama was equally poor. Academic pressures were, of course, strong and the pursuit of A-levels at good grades was a prime objective. I cannot help feeling though that the incidence of self-pitying, dissatisfied VIth formers must have had a damaging effect on the GCE results.

During this period the headmaster, Michael Thornley, had to deal with a variety of discipline problems of a fundamental nature. I shall always admire the way in which he dealt with some of the issues that arose. At no stage did he acquiesce in the demands for VIth-form bars, the scrapping of uniform, the VIth-form house, the abolition of compulsory games or the wearing of long hair. I believe he preserved a great deal of the ethos of the school and made it much easier for the more liberal and progressive changes that have been made in recent years to be carried out in the present climate of co-operation.

I remember well a silent lunch and a refusal of the school to sing during a chapel service. Both were organized demonstrations in protest at the school regulation on the length of hair—no longer touching the collar.

The communication between the senior boys and the younger members of staff was generally very unsatisfactory. How different to the excellent spirit of co-operation that exists now. This would seem to be quite the most significant change over the last five years: the relationship between masters and boys has improved beyond recognition.

The prefectorial system went through a radical change at about this time. In 1969 there was considerably less of a barrier in the social hierarchy within a boarding house than there was in 1963. The idea of senior boys taking responsibility for junior ones had far less significance and in many cases it was obvious that prefects did not uphold regulations themselves or indeed pay more than lip service to the functions that housemasters were requiring of them. To me this was all very depressing. Drugs too were an inevitable threat and Sedbergh had its share of cases. Some were detected and others were not. Upon reflection I can only explain the bizarre behaviour of some individuals by assuming that they must have been on drugs.

The picture that emerges is one of considerable unpleasantness. It would not be an exaggeration to say that in those first few years of my new career as a schoolmaster it was remarkably depressing. The comparison with the atmosphere in the school when I left it in 1963 was not at all favourable. It is certain that I must have felt it more acutely than a number of my colleagues by the very nature of being an old boy. It was to the eternal credit of Michael Thornley and his staff that the storm and upheavals of those few years were weathered, and that during the next decade a complete reversal took place so that now the atmosphere at Sedbergh is better than ever before. Enthusiastic participation in all sorts of activities has produced a climate in the school where change and innovation can be made with care and insight; a climate that all can be pleased and proud of.

I have quoted John Morris at length not because his account is exceptional but because it is typical. The same story, with only minor variations, could have been told of almost any public school in the late sixties.

The second comment on the mood of the times is made in Lindsay Anderson's film *If*. The film, released in 1968, is set in a public school and by means of satire and fantasy illustrates some of the more gruesome aspects of the traditional boarding school.

The sharpness of the satire and the rebellious climax persuaded many headmasters that the film was subversive of all that public schools stood for. Most pupils probably saw it that way too. But the film was a work of imagination, not principally a piece of social propaganda. Its appearance in 1968, when unrest in the schools was gathering momentum, was fortuitous; it would have appeared earlier if the authors had not found it so difficult to obtain backers. The original script—called *Crusaders*—had been written by David Sherwin and John Howlett, drawing on their own experiences as boys at Tonbridge. No one in Britain would back the film financially because the story was thought to have no appeal overseas. One producer disliked the satire on public schools so much that he thought the authors ought to be horse-whipped. Even when Lindsay Anderson agreed to work on the film it had to be made with American money. In the event it was more successful abroad than in Britain, though it was banned for a time in Czechoslovakia.

There were those who would have liked to see it banned in Britain too. Nothing more accurately reveals the value of the film as a reflection of the mood of the times than the fact that many public school headmasters were very worried about the effect the film might have on their pupils. Lindsay Anderson may have seen the film as an allegory of the tensions between anarchy and order, between traditionalism and individualism, but these were precisely the tensions that were being so painfully exposed in the schools when the film was distributed. However fortuitous its timing, *If* both mirrored and fuelled the unrest and disaffection in the schools.

What made the headmaster flinch when he slipped into the local cinema during afternoon school, was that however exaggerated and 'unfair' the film's sketches from public school life, he recognized the truth in them: the hearty but hollow chapel service; the ineffectual chaplain, probing a boy's erotic daydreams one minute and commanding the Cadet Corps the next; the weak housemaster giving his prefects a free hand to organize a sadistic beating; the bullying; the throbbing sexuality of adolescence expressed as heterosexual fantasy and homosexual reality; and, among the masters, mediocrity masquerading as eccentricity.

The unkindest cut and the most perceptive portrait was that of the headmaster. He is portrayed not as a reactionary old buffer but as a smooth younger man who has 'enlightened' attitudes and who thinks he understands the disaffected and bolshie boys. Some of his more fatuous speeches were direct quotations from a book by an Eton master, J. D. R. McConnell, *Eton—How it Works*, published in the previous year. Faced with rebels who have just shot the chaplain on the Cadet Corps field day, the headmaster speaks McConnell's lines:

One thing is certain; short hair is not an indication of merit. So often I have noticed that the hair rebels step into the breach when there is a crisis—whether it be a fire in the house or an invitation to give a party of slum children seven days in the country. Of course there are limits. Scruffiness of any kind is deplorable. . . .

Not surprisingly, at the film's rebellious climax, the headmaster is the first to be shot as he calls out to the boys with the sub-machine guns in their hands that he understands them. Like the militant boys, Anderson and his scriptwriters spotted that the headmasters of the time were caught in a period of ideological transition; they lacked confidence in the old public school values and found it difficult to justify a number of the restrictions and compulsions they imposed. But neither they nor the public schools as a whole had developed a new ideology, so that changes were made pragmatically and piecemeal in response to demands and pressures. It is to these changes that we must now turn.

6

Response to the Challenge of the Sixties

A Question of Relationships

In the consideration of periods of change it is easy to overlook the element of continuity. If a man who had entered his public school in 1960 could repeat the process in 1980 he would probably find more that was familiar than unfamiliar. He would note superficial differences: a television to help while away the long wet Sunday afternoon and a calculator to ease the passage of his mathematics prep. He would also find that there were fewer occasions and events he was compelled to attend so that he had more time to himself or time on his hands. He would note a new emphasis on academic achievement. What would strike him more forcibly was that the relations between people were different to those of twenty years before: masters less distant, older boys less brutal, his contemporaries less intolerant of eccentricity, the school less isolated from the surrounding community. Whether he would agree with his new headmaster that the school was a much happier place than it had been in 1960 is less certain. The inclination of headmasters to present bland generalizations as acknowledged facts would be one thing that had not changed.

Headmasters have no doubt that their schools have changed for the better. It is axiomatic among them that Lindsay Anderson's *If* is now so dated as to be a period piece. They are no longer afraid of its impact on their pupils; when it was shown on television in 1979, the independent schools hardly noticed. The headmasters, over-anxious in the late sixties, are now perhaps over-confident. The world of *If* has not disappeared. The tensions between anarchy and order, between traditionalism and individualism are still there; they are bound to be in any society and especially in the closed society of an institution. The fact that the tensions are less obvious now may be attributed partly to the changed economic climate: the need to find a secure job with the right status and income leaves the public school boy little time or inclination to improve the world or challenge authority. But the easing of these tensions also owes something to the fact that the balance has been adjusted in favour of the individual and if not exactly in favour of anarchy, then at least in favour of choice and variety. Whether the public schools are really happier places may be endlessly debated but few who know the schools would disagree with the claim that the quality of relationships now makes it less likely that a boy will be unhappy for long.

Relations between boys and the school authorities
Relations between school pupils and their teachers adjust to the changing relationship between adults and young people in society. There are, however, permanent features. It could hardly be otherwise when the age groups and the nature of the exercise remain essentially the same. There will always be latent hostility between boys and masters. Teachers who believe it is possible to remove altogether the feeling of Them and Us deceive themselves. However open and informal the relationship, the teacher is still the enemy to some boys and to all boys at some times. It is part game and part serious, rather like the popular conception of the relationship between British officers and German guards in a prisoner of war camp. This mixture of play and deadly earnest is caught in a schoolboy poem of the early sixteenth century:

> I wold my master were an hare,
> And all his bokes howndes were,
> And I myself a joly hontere;
> To blow my horn I would not spare,
> For if he were dede I wold not care!

Schoolboy attitudes do not change much over the centuries.

Nor does their desire to outwit authority. A fifteenth-century schoolmaster complained: 'As soon as I am come into the school this fellow goeth to make water.' It is the oldest trick in the book. Just as boys enjoyed outwitting authority, so they were suspicious of one of their number who appeared to be too keen on winning authority's approval. When my twin sons started at their boarding school in 1980 they found that any boy who gave the right answer too often in class was likely to be greeted by sucking noises all round the room; medieval schoolboys would have understood the signal immediately.

So it is against the background of such more or less fixed elements that the changes in relationships between masters and boys in independent schools should be seen.

At almost any point in the history of the independent schools it is possible to find someone arguing for an improvement of relationships between teachers and taught. In medieval and early modern times the familiar complaint was that the schoolmaster was 'a little despotic emperor' who wielded absolute and brutal authority over his pupils; the natural tension in the situation was exacerbated by the contempt of well-to-do boys for underpaid ushers. In the nineteenth century the status of the schoolmaster improved, though he remained in a social limbo between the wealthy, whose children he educated and the poor, whose ignorance he despised. In his relations with the boys he was somewhat less brutal but still distant; informal social intercourse was frowned upon because it might threaten discipline and was inconsistent with the dignity of the master. When Edward Bowen, who was to become the most celebrated assistant master of his day, joined the Harrow staff in 1859 he was reprimanded by senior colleagues for walking along the street in conversation with two boys. Bowen satirized the attitude of the older men in a long poem where the masters appear as gods and the boys as earthly mortals. The older gods declare that the suggestion that relations with mortals should be more informal is 'Rank treason discussed in the name of reform'. Nor are they pleased when Mercury proposes an alternative to godlike aloofness:

> But suppose we turn *human*; the deified tell us
> That men are not monsters but excellent fellows.

The argument continued for a hundred years. By the 1960s, relations *had* become less formal; masters had become more 'human', contacts with boys more friendly. What happened in response to the challenge of youth at the end of the decade was that the process was taken a step further. When the unrest subsided in the early seventies, masters and boys found that they could approach one another with less fear and less suspicion on both sides. For the first time in the history of these schools it became common practice for masters to call boys by their first names. The fixed elements in the relationship remained; they had been modified by the more flexible and informal attitude of the school authorities.

This change in relationships both made possible and was made possible by a new attitude to the traditional compulsions and restrictions. More informal relationships and a less regimented lifestyle emerged together from the confusion of the time. In most public schools the traditional compulsions were eased rather than abolished. Neither boys nor staff wanted too much voluntarism. Too much freedom and leisure meant boredom for the boys and trouble for the staff—necessary routine not only helped to pass the time, it provided the framework that held the life of the community in place.

So in most schools compulsory attendance at chapel was not abolished but reduced: one compulsory service on Sunday instead of two; or a choice of services, holy communion for the saints and congregational service for the sinners, an arrangement that allowed the more enterprising boys to miss both. During the week compulsory attendance either disappeared altogether or was reduced by means of some more or less random formula such as every other day. House prayers, a splendidly pagan occasion at which boys, cooped up with their prep for what seemed to them long hours, could let themselves go with their favourite hymns, were also dropped by most schools at this time.

Other compulsions were similarly modified or allowed to fade away. Boys were allowed more choice in the games and sports they wished to pursue. When I joined the staff at Harrow in 1955, almost all boys played cricket in the summer term; a few were allowed to swim because such an eccentric and socially downmarket sport posed no threat to the supremacy of Harrow's great game. By 1979, Harrovians could choose from a list of half a dozen sports including tennis, athletics and golf.

The Combined Cadet Force also lost its monopoly: boys could opt out—at least in the sixth form—to do the Duke of Edinburgh Award Scheme or some form of community service. They could not, however, choose to do nothing or to work at their books. It was choice rather than the voluntary principle that headmasters were introducing. Greater choice in uniform came too, but no public school abolished uniform altogether. Quite apart from other considerations, the boys enjoyed having the opportunity of wearing the wide variety of house and school colours that were still awarded in the form of ties, scarves and badges. Points of friction remained. Though boys were now allowed to wear their own clothes after school, in most cases they had to put on uniform to go into the town. School uniform had been first introduced in the eighteenth century as a means of facilitating the out-of-school surveillance of the boys; at one charity school, for example, the boys wore 'blue caps to enable people to observe their behaviour abroad'. Given the behaviour of some of their pupils, headmasters might have preferred them to be anonymous when they went into the town, but in most schools this aspect of the old compulsion remained intact.

The easing of compulsions was accompanied by the relaxing of the restrictions on a boy's movements. Before the 'revolution' these restrictions could be as extensive and detailed as the dress regulations. The restrictions on a Harrow boy's movements in the early sixties included:

The following acts are permanently forbidden:
1. Going beyond—
   (a) The bottom of Peterborough Road.
   (b) The bottom of Grove Hill.

(c) The bottom of Roxborough Park.
(d) The Bessborough Road at the point where the Bessborough Field ends.
2. Going to the King's Head Hotel.
3. Going to any railway station or its approaches.
4. Standing still on any railway bridge or going on the line.
5. Loitering in the churchyard on Sundays, or standing in groups at the outer doors of Houses or outside the Chapel doors.
6. Buying any articles (except newspapers) in the streets.
7. Keeping dogs or taking dogs out.
8. Walking more than three abreast up and down the streets or London Road.
9. Going in any public conveyance without permission.

The headmaster of Harrow also issued instructions to the owners or managers of the shops that were in bounds. These included:

1. Care must be taken in obtaining shop assistants of good character.
2. No shop to which boys are allowed to go must be left in charge of young girls.

Leave to be away from the school was very tightly controlled. Boys were allowed to attend the weddings 'of their own family or other near relations' or the funerals of 'relatives or intimate friends'. Even the visits of parents were the subject of regulations:

With the leave of his House Master a boy may go out with his parents for a drive when they visit him on Sunday provided that the drive is in the direction away from London and that it does not entail the missing of any School obligation. The boy must remain in School (Sunday) dress.

Similar restrictions existed in other boarding schools. They underwent a marked change in the early seventies. Boys were given greater freedom from bounds and in most schools were allowed to go home much more frequently. With the introduction of a half-term Exeat (in some schools for as long as a week) and the right to claim two or more shorter Exeats during the term, boys could go home as often as once a month. One or two schools introduced a system that amounted to fortnightly boarding. The fear that contact with home would undermine the spirit of boarding was soon proved to be unfounded, though not all parents welcomed the change; the expense of travel and the sheer nuisance of having to fetch and deliver their sons at the weekend made some parents critical of the new arrangements.

The traditional restriction on smoking was not modified. Smoking remained an offence except in those Roman Catholic schools where it was already established as a sixth-form privilege. If other headmasters were inclined to give way to pressure for a similar privilege to be granted in their school, the report on the connection between smoking and health provided a timely stiffening of their resolve. Determination to stand firm on smoking was strengthened by the spread of the use of cannabis. Headmasters did not claim that cigarette smoking necessarily led on to cannabis smoking, but they noted that the boys who were in trouble with the latter had almost invariably been in trouble with the former. New rules forbidding the use or possession of illegal drugs represented one area in which the school's policy became more restrictive; but while this usually had the effect of reducing the risk of drug abuse within the school, the simultaneous extension of Exeats increased the risk that boys from boarding schools would indulge in the fashionable vices at weekend parties. When schools in the seventies said that they no longer had a drug problem, it could mean that they had managed to push the problem on to the parents.

The schools' approach to the problem of drinking was different. Going to pubs or smuggling alcohol in the boarding house had long been both strictly forbidden and frequently practised. Headmasters now sought to modernize the schools' attitude by the classic public school device of turning an offence into a privilege. School bars were established, open to sixth formers or to boys over seventeen. Usually run by boys, with a master as treasurer, and only opened at carefully prescribed hours, the bars were probably successful in reducing the amount of illegal drinking. They certainly provided the headmaster with a clear justification for punishing those boys who still insisted on visiting pubs. The bars were a tacit recognition by the school authorities that their boys were no strangers to alcohol. With more money in their pockets, more alcohol available at home and a society unwilling to enforce drinking laws as far as young people were concerned, public school boys joined in the national boom in teenage drinking.

The picture, then, is of a more flexible and less regimented society. The changes so far described hardly justify the concept of 'revolution' but they did significantly affect the life of the boys. Nor were they any less valuable for having been made on pragmatic rather than dogmatic grounds; ideals and principles are not necessarily the best basis for extending human happiness. The headmasters who eased the compulsions and restrictions of the old-style public school certainly had mixed motives. Weekend Exeats brought home and school closer together and that was recognized as an improvement; but they also made it easier for schools to cope with the weekends, when fewer staff were prepared to leave their families to supervise or organize the boys. Similarly, the concession that allowed boys to opt out of the Combined Cadet Force reflected the difficulty headmasters had in finding young masters with military experience who could be pressed into service as officers. In these and other areas, changes owed something to the logistics of staffing as well as to belief in the virtue of greater freedom and choice.

A striking example of the difficulty of discovering what motivation lay behind changes in the independent schools in this period is the case of corporal punishment. No one doubts that its use has declined, in some schools disappeared altogether, or that this has altered the relations between masters and boys. But precisely why it has declined is far from clear. There is little evidence that parents objected or that the headmasters themselves had scruples. As for the boys, they would appear to have been as ambivalent as ever. There was never any protest against corporal punishment as there had been in previous centuries and as there was against restrictions on the length of hair. Boys did not particularly like being beaten but they wanted to know what the school would substitute as an alternative. As the use of corporal punishment declined, the authorities substituted rustication, that is the sending home of the culprit for two or three weeks. Some boys would have preferred to be beaten: it was over quickly and it did not involve their parents; nor were they much interested in the psychological overtones that worried the reformers.

There is something to be said for the view that headmasters discouraged the use of corporal punishment, particularly by boys, because they were worried about the public schools' unfavourable image at the time. Though apologists argued that the brutal flogging scene in *If* bore no relation to the truth, the public thought otherwise. Privately, HMC recognized this. The list that HMC drew up in the early sixties of 'ten popular myths that must be scotched', included the myth that public schools 'foster bullying and sadism, particularly through corporal punishment and fagging'.

It was not that the British public was against corporal punishment as such. Though it had been abolished as a weapon in the hands of the courts by the Criminal Justice Act of 1948, there were regular demands for its reinstatement to deal with young thugs. It was also widely used in maintained schools. But its use in public schools provoked an altogether different kind of popular feeling which had more to do with class than psychology. The prefect wielding a cane seemed to be as out of keeping with a democratic society as an aristocratic cavalry officer dispersing a trade union demonstration.

The flogging and fagging image did worry headmasters and it was no coincidence that both practices declined at the same time. But to attribute the decline in the use of corporal punishment solely to a concern for public relations is to oversimplify. The interaction between the relaxing of restrictions and the development of a more open and informal style of relationship created a climate that was unsympathetic to physical punishment. The cane was used less and less because headmasters and housemasters felt less and less inclined to use it. Corporal punishment was regarded as out of place rather than wrong in principle. As a result it was retained in most schools only as a 'last resort', a policy advocated, incidentally, by John Locke in the seventeenth century. In other schools it just fell into disuse and has not been revived. Ironically, in view of the history of protest on this issue, the campaign against corporal punishment is now concentrated on the maintained schools.

The consensus among the headmasters is that all these changes in the relations between the school authorities and the boys have made the schools better and happier places. It is easy to be sceptical of such optimism, which is reminiscent of the optimism of the Whig historians: the history of the public schools is the history of increasing tolerance and humanity as the old regime surrenders to enlightenment. But if we use the rather less imprecise criterion of unhappiness we must look at the changing relations among the boys themselves, because cases of acute unhappiness were more likely to be caused by the way the boys treated each other than by the way they were treated by the school authorities.

Relations between boys

One important change in relations between boys in this period was the modification of the role of the prefect or monitor. In the public school of the early sixties it still mattered in the day-to-day life of a young boy that he gave the right impression to the prefects. His relations with masters were secondary; the masters were the commissioned officers and at the end of the day they retired to the officers' mess. But the prefects were the non-commissioned officers, the sergeants and corporals, who were ever present and whom it was essential to impress with one's willingness to obey.

The idea of prefects is as old as the public schools themselves. The Founder's statutes at Winchester included the following instruction:

> In each of the lower chambers let there be at least three Scholars of good character, more advanced than the rest in age, discretion and knowledge, who may superintend their chamber fellows in their studies, and oversee them diligently,

and may from time to time certify and inform the Warden, Sub-Warden, and Head Master respecting their behaviour, conversation and progress in study.

The role of the prefect developed in a way that reflected both the degree of supervision the school authorities were prepared to give and the way society outside the school was run. However closed the boarding school institution might be, it could not help being influenced in its methods of government by what was acceptable in the outside world. In the sixteenth and seventeenth centuries, the master appointed prefects to assist him in checking and disciplining the other boys. Unknown to these prefects, he also appointed 'clandestine' monitors to act as 'privy spies' both on the boys and on the prefects themselves. It was a style of control that Walsingham and Robert Cecil would have approved. At the end of the seventeenth century, when Dr Busby had made Westminster so successful and fashionable a school that the upper classes were persuaded to abandon the private tutor and send their sons, the role of the prefect changed. Aristocratic young men had no intention of being mere instruments of the master—they took power into their own hands and transformed the prefect body into a ruling oligarchy with powers of beating and fagging. The eighteenth century was the hey-day of unbridled prefectorial power which tyrannized boys and ushers alike.

It was against this form of political government that Dr Arnold rebelled. He disliked the corrupt and tyrannical oligarchies as much as he disliked everything else about the godless eighteenth century. His achievement was to purge the prefect's role of its corruption, inspire it with his own ideals and return it to its original purpose as an adjunct of the master's power. Once again the prefect's role tended to reflect the style of leadership favoured in society, in particular the style of leadership required to control a far-flung empire: reliable young men who knew and accepted their place in the chain of command, capable of taking responsibility at a young age but not likely to cause trouble by showing too much imagination.

The re-establishment of the prefect's role as a link between masters and boys, also helped to improve the status of the assistant master. He, too, was part of the chain of command. But in almost all public schools it was still the prefect who had the greater power and prestige. There is a scene in *If* where a prefect indicates to a new master that it is time he went to bed; the relationship is exactly that between a long-serving company sergeant-major and a raw subaltern. Masters who saw the film would have noted the accuracy of every nuance in the exchange.

By the early sixties, the role of the prefect had changed in detail but not in substance over the last hundred years. Kalton's 1966 survey found that in three-quarters of the boarding schools prefects still had the power to beat and that in two-thirds of the schools fagging was still in operation. It is interesting to compare the power of senior boys with regard to corporal punishment at Harrow in 1866 and a hundred years later.

In 1866, the powers of the Harrow school monitors were outlined as follows:

> Punishments inflicted by the Monitors, as recognized representatives of the School, are considered of more efficacy than if inflicted by a Master. Such punishments are impositions, which are rarely set—extra fagging, if a Boy is subject to it; reprimand; and caning, which is not restricted to particular offences, but is seldom inflicted unless something of impertinence or of a deliberate character is involved. The heaviest punishment, which would be inflicted for gross bullying, is a 'public whopping' or caning by the Captain in presence of the whole School. A boy may appeal either to the Monitors in a body, or to the Head Master, and the appeal suspends the punishment, and if the Head Master supports the Monitor, must either submit or leave the school. Such appeals are very rare.

A hundred years later the school monitors' power to use corporal punishment was defined in terms that were not dissimilar:

(a) A Monitors' Meeting has authority to cane officially,

provided that the sentence be affirmed by a two-thirds majority, that there be the right of appeal to the Head Master, and that the Head Master be informed beforehand should this right not be exercised.

(b) The Head of the School, on report of another Monitor or in extraordinary cases on his own responsibility, has authority to cane, but there must be another Monitor present. This authority is not given to other individual Monitors.

(c) The Captain of the Eleven has authority to cane for neglect of cricket fagging, but a Monitor must not be present.

It may be argued that a school such as Harrow was peculiarly resistant to reform and therefore not typical. When the Public Schools Commission started work at the end of 1965, headmasters claimed that the practice of the beating of boys by boys was dying out but Kalton's figures make a nonsense of this claim. Not for the first or last time, the headmasters of public schools were inclined to exaggerate the extent to which a practice that offended public opinion was disappearing.

The impact of the 'teenage revolution' on the role of the prefect was profound. It made senior boys much less willing to identify with the masters' authority; but whereas in the eighteenth century this had been because the boys had had no intention of sharing power with socially inferior ushers, in the late sixties it was because they did not wish to exercise power at all. The crisis of authority affected prefects in schools just as it did a whole range of other roles in society. In some schools boys now refused to accept the position of prefect, though interestingly enough there appear to have been few such cases; boys wanted the privileges without the responsibility and without having to play a role that would separate them from their fellows.

As we have seen, a few headmasters such as Frank Fisher had already abolished the prefects' power to beat. In the early sixties others followed suit. Ian Beer was appointed headmaster of Ellesmere College in 1961 at the age of thirty-one. Coming from John Dancy's Marlborough, Beer found Ellesmere's approach to prefectorial power archaic. The prefects carried canes (as in Lindsay Anderson's *If*) and were free to use them on cheeky and unruly boys. Like concentration camp guards they walked up and down the dinner queue, canes twitching, ready to pounce on any boy who broke the rule of silence. In the large room where the boys did their prep in the evenings the prefects sat on raised platforms waiting for disobedience. The prefects told Beer that if he took away their canes and their right to beat, a riot would break out. Beer ignored their warnings; there was no riot.

It was fifteen years before ISIS could claim that the beating of boys by boys was a thing of the past and in many cases it had been the prefects themselves who had rejected the power or allowed it to fall into disuse.

When headmasters found that they could no longer rely on the co-operation of senior boys, they were tempted to experiment with what were thought to be more democratic forms of government. Instead of appointing prefects himself, the headmaster made the position subject to election; or he merged the prefectorial body in a newly constituted School Council. At Bishops Stortford College, the young headmaster, Peter Rowe, set up a School Council in 1966. The Council blended prefects, who were still appointed by the headmaster, with the elected representatives of the houses. The Council was deliberative and advisory; the headmaster still made the decisions but he hoped the Council would keep him more in touch with opinion in the school and provide a forum for open discussion of school problems. 'There seems every reason to suppose,' the school's official history commented in 1969, 'that the School Council will make an increasingly important contribution to the running of the School.' But when a few years later Rowe's successor quietly buried the Council, there were no protests.

The demand for greater participation, so characteristic of the late sixties, led to surprisingly few experiments of this sort; and those that did occur were short-lived. Once again the majority of boys were not much interested in what the militants called 'school democracy'. But while experiments with greater participation made little impact, the change in the role of the prefect did and seemed likely to establish a new style of leadership by senior boys that would last.

As had happened in the past, it was a question of the style adapting to the accepted modes of leadership in society. Many British institutions at this time went in for extensive heart-searching about the nature of their government. It was not just the universities and the schools. As one Anglican priest put it: 'The hierarchical model is no longer relevant.' But institutions found that it was impossible to dispense with hierarchy altogether and independent schools were no exception. In the schools the hierarchy loosened but did not disappear. Younger boys not only approached prefects without awe but called them by their Christian names. The prefects could no longer beat or demand that a younger boy fag for them. Fagging had by no means been universal but it had been the norm in boarding schools. Now it began to disappear either by a gradual reduction of the prefect's power or by a single act of abolition by the headmaster. Housemasters and senior boys were not always keen to see it go. At Eton it was not abolished until 1980 because Michael McCrum had publicly committed himself to waiting until there was a two-thirds majority in favour of abolition at the housemasters' meeting.

Prefects were still appointed by the headmaster—the public ritual surviving in most schools—but their role was now closer to that of the friendly neighbourhood policeman than the platoon sergeant. They could and did exercise authority, checking minor breaches of school rules and supervising public occasions such as school meals, but they were no longer feared. They could expect much less automatic obedience and respect. They had to convince boys of the good sense of what was being required of them, a skill that many people in positions of authority in Britain were having to learn.

Schools functioned no less efficiently though more re-sponsibility fell on the masters, particularly the housemasters. Whereas in the past senior boys had effectively run a number of the school activities, notably the games, the tendency now was for these to be run by masters with boys helping but not taking the ultimate responsibility. On the other hand there were some activities, such as community service and drama, where senior boys took more responsibility not less. In some schools, the most senior boys were allowed to opt out of positions of responsibility altogether by moving to a sixth-form house, leaving the prefectorial role to the next layer down.

The consequences of this change in role of the prefect were two-fold: the work load on the staff increased and relations between boys became more open and friendly and less restricted by status and seniority. It was no longer the case that a boy made his friends from within his own age group and his own house. The old taboos about going into another boy's house or mixing with boys younger or older than yourself disappeared.

Those who had known the old style of prefect regretted that senior boys would no longer experience what was believed to be training for leadership; but the training implicit in the old-style prefect's role was not only out of date by the sixties but arguably had been for a long time. The young man who assumed that because he had been a prefect at his public school he had the qualities of a leader could be said to have done considerable damage in society, not least in the area of industrial relations. The country as well as the schools would benefit from the disappearance of this anachronism.

Simultaneously with the changing role of the prefect, there occurred a marked decline in the incidence of bullying. Dr Arnold had seen authority in the hands of responsible senior boys as a means of 'avoiding the evils of anarchy . . . . the lawless tyranny of physical strength'. It will be remembered that the heaviest penalty in the hands of the Harrow monitors in 1866— the 'public whopping'—was inflicted for 'gross bullying'. The school authorities undoubtedly hoped that the old-style prefect would provide an effective deterrent to the bullies, for whom corporal punishment was universally regarded as the appropriate punishment. Yet the fact remains that the decline in ritual and casual bullying of younger boys by older coincided with the reduction of both prefectorial power and corporal punishment. It was not perhaps a simple case of cause and effect: less prefectorial power and physical punishment results in less bullying. All these aspects of public school life were affected by the more gentle and informal mood of the time. But the loosening of the hierarchy and the outlawing of beating by boys, did help to ensure that bullying would not return in the less gentle and more violent years at the end of the seventies. What defenders of the old regime in public schools are reluctant to admit is that there was a connection, however difficult to trace, between the strict hierarchy with its petty tyrannies of dress and custom, the use of physical punishment and the incidence of organized bullying of the younger boys. It is this organized bullying that has virtually disappeared; when it does occur the new-style prefects are more likely to stop it than the old because they do not accept it as part of the public school life. It would be wrong to give the impression that life in public schools is now all sweetness and light; in any school, boarding or day, independent or maintained, the boys and girls are capable of harassment or cruelty. That has not changed. What has changed is that at the independent boarding schools bullying is no longer built into the system and a timid boy is now less likely to be made unhappy in this way than at any time in the past. It would need a remarkably misanthropic critic to argue that that was not a significant improvement.

Another aspect of the relations between boys that changed in this period was the sexual one. Headmasters may have regarded it as a myth that public schools 'promote homosexuality' but in this they were being disingenuous; they knew that adolescent homosexuality could flourish in that closed, masculine world, so much so that words with a heterosexual meaning in the outside world, words such as 'tart' and 'lusher', were used homosexually in the single-sex boarding school. It can remember a Harrow housemaster in the late fifties referring to one of his younger boys as 'the school tart'.

In the sixties there were a number of *causes célèbres*. In one of the most famous boarding schools, the headmaster uncovered what was in effect organized prostitution. A senior boy who was head of his house and a school prefect procured younger boys as partners for his friends at a price. When the racket was exposed, the boy's housemaster would not believe that his head of house had been the organizer; he was a boy in whom he had had absolute trust.

Much homosexual activity never came to the notice of the authorities though it was almost always widely known among the boys. Masters preferred not to know too much. It was seldom if ever openly discussed, though there was a fierce debate at Harrow about whether boys should be allowed to wear swimming costumes in the school's open-air swimming bath, the advocates of nudity claiming that a young boy in swimming trunks was more erotically attractive to older boys than if he was in the nude. But how much homosexual activity occurred and how damaging it was to the boys' chances of making mature heterosexual relationships as adults it is impossible to say. The evidence is too subjective and anecdotal to be regarded as hard fact. The *impression* is that in all the single-sex boarding schools homosexual activity was at some periods commonplace. What Robert Graves wrote in *Goodbye to All That* about Charterhouse before the First World War was probably still true of public schools after the Second:

> In English preparatory and public schools romance is necessarily homosexual. The opposite sex is despised and hated, treated as something obscene. Many boys never recover from this perversion. I only recovered by a shock at the age of twenty-one. For everyone born a homosexual there were at least ten permanent pseudo-homosexuals made by the public school system. And nine of these ten are as honourably chaste and sentimental as I was.

The negative, even hostile attitude towards women was still a feature of the traditional boarding schools in the early sixties. A heavy, masculine pall hung over the institution. All members of the opposite sex, from the headmaster's wife to the maids in the kitchen, were treated as peripheral to the life of the school. When I became headmaster of Taunton School in 1966, my wife wanted to attend the school chapel service on the first Sunday. The chaplain and housemasters were taken aback. My predecessor had been a bachelor and the services in chapel were looked upon as male occasions. My wife ignored them and took her place but the atmosphere in the chapel was electric. One might have been introducing a striptease dancer to the Athenaeum. Fortunately, there was a splendid senior master who, with his wife, gave us support and the tradition of the all-male service was broken. But it was a reminder of how frightened of women some public schools could be.

The real danger of this hostility and fear was not perhaps that the boys would grow up to be pseudo-homosexuals but that in some way their emotional development would be stunted. Like long-term prisoners, the public school boys had to feed their sexual appetitie on a diet of fantasy and masturbation. The characteristic 'love affair' was a romantic one, seldom involving physical contact. The effect of life in a single-sex boarding school was to turn the adolescent sex drive in on itself. At the same time the rough institutional life forced boys to suppress any emotion that was tender or affectionate. E. M. Forster's public school boys with 'underdeveloped hearts' may not have been universal but they were certainly common. In that tight little world of taboos and almost total lack of privacy, survival depended on being able to hide your emotions. As a result some—perhaps many—boys found that as adults they were incapable of giving themselves freely in love. The risk was too great. Their emotions were like the inmates of a concentration camp: they had been confined so harshly for so long that when the chance came to go free, they hardly dared to do so. This rather than homosexuality or pseudo-homosexuality was the likely psychological aftermath of the single-sex boarding school.

It would be ludicrous to suggest that all public school boys grew up emotionally or sexually crippled; but in the old-style boarding school there was a risk of this happening. Now the impression is that the risk has been very much reduced. Yet inevitably the evidence is still largely a matter of assumption rather than knowledge. We make the assumption from the following facts.

The all-pervading masculinity of the institution has been diluted. A higher proportion of the masters are married. Their wives may still feel somewhat peripheral but they are more involved in the life of the school. Their children run freely about the campus. There is more contact with nearby girls' schools; it is rare now for boys to take the female parts in school plays. There are 2,750 girl boarders and 6,000 day girls in HMC schools, some of the day girls being in schools that are mainly boarding. The boys have greater access to the outside world and the new system of Exeats enables them to maintain heterosexual relationships. It is a reasonable assumption that these changes have reduced homosexual activity and the risk of warping emotional development. But it is too soon to be sure what the long-term effect of such changes is. One Marlborough housemaster argued that the introduction of girl boarders at Marlborough had possibly increased homosexual activity because it had stimulated erotic feeling without giving an opportunity for most boys to express that feeling in a heterosexual way. It also remains true that in the single-sex boarding schools the attitude of the authorities to the opposite sex is cautious; they have had to come to terms with girls but only with reluctance. Girls are bussed in for the sixth-form dance, carefully rounded up after the event and bussed out again. It is an innovation that reminds one of the more enlightened prisons where prisoners' wives are allowed to come and sleep with their husbands once a month. In such schools the boys are more likely to lead double lives than homosexual ones: girl-friends in the holidays and—as the BBC film on Radley made explicit—masturbation during the term.

It would be wishful thinking to suppose that the single-sex boarding school will ever be entirely free from the risks of some degree of sexual disorientation. Headmasters have recognized this and have taken steps to reduce the risk. The majority are still not convinced that the advantages of co-education outweigh the loss of the school's traditional character; and they are reluctant to introduce cosmetic co-education, that is a few girls in the sixth form, because they suspect that such unbalanced numbers—forty girls perhaps in a boys' school of six hundred—may be just as disorientating for both boys and girls as the single-sex situation. Headmistresses are inclined to agree with them and strongly reject the validity of the concept of using a handful of girls to solve the long-established problems of the boys' boarding schools. This is not the least of the reasons why the introduction of girls to boys' public schools has been the most controversial innovation of this period.

Cosmetic and real co-education

In the early sixties no public school was co-educational. There were independent co-educational schools, the best known of which was Bedales, but it was precisely because such schools admitted girls as well as boys that they were regarded not as public schools but as experimental and outside the main tradition. In 1979, sixty out of the 210 schools in the Headmasters' Conference admitted girls and of these twenty-six had gone fully co-educational from the age of eleven or thirteen. As a result there were some 9,000 girls in HMC schools, representing about 7 per cent of the total number of pupils. The percentage of girls was small but it was increasing every year.

The process had not been two-way: though some girls' public schools opened their doors to boys, the boys had been reluctant to apply. In 1979, there were only thirty-nine boys in GSA schools out of a total population of 75,000. What had changed, therefore, was that a number of boys' schools had followed Bedales and become co-educational schools and a larger number had, for a variety of reasons, decided to admit girls to the sixth form.

The headmistresses of girls' independent schools were convinced that the headmasters' motives had little to do with educational philosophy. They accused headmasters of being motivated by a shortfall in the number of boys or by a superficial and ill-thought-out belief that boys' schools would somehow be healthier for having girls around. There is little doubt that some of the schools that opted for cosmetic co-education in the sixth form acted for economic reasons; and it is possible that some headmasters, and in particular some governing bodies, gave only cursory consideration to the social and educational consequences of what they were doing. We shall consider the economic and recruiting factors in Chapter 7. Here we are concerned with the other possible motives and with the effect of the admission of girls both on the schools and on the girls themselves.

The first headmaster to admit girls to what had formerly been a boys' public school was John Dancy of Marlborough. The motive was not economic. Dancy was one of the very few headmasters who had a clear idea of what needed to be changed in the public schools and of how that change might be effected. He introduced girls to Marlborough in 1969. In 1979 I asked him what his motives had been and he replied:

> You might be interested to know what finally pushed me in that direction. It was a chance remark by Bernard Williams* when he came to Marlborough on one of the visitations which the first Public Schools Commission carried out. We were discussing the poor prospects of getting any social de-segregation of public schools and he said roughly this: 'I can't understand why you don't get on with what is easily within your power, the sexual desegregation of Marlborough.' I did, therefore, see the admission of girls as being a continuance, if on a different line, of the general direction in which the Commission was moving.
>
> The other main motive which was in my mind (I am not sure whether it got there before the arrival of the girls or soon after) was the desire to render permanent the changes that had come over public schools during the previous decade. I mean particularly the jettisoning of most of the remaining barbarities and absurdities which were thought (and still are in some quarters) to be central to the public school ethos. What I feared, round about 1969, was a fascist backlash, and I felt that girls would consolidate the liberal position so that the changes were irreversible. It would, I suppose, be possible to test this hypothesis by seeing whether there are now any detectable differences between the ethos of schools which remained single sex and those which have accepted a substantial minority of girls.

Dancy's motives—desegregation and the consolidation of liberal reforms—are also the ones that other headmasters give,

* A member of the Public Schools Commission 1965–8 and Knightsbridge Professor of Philosophy at Cambridge University.

though in some cases they speak of the arrival of girls facilitating rather than consolidating the reforms. There is no reason to believe that the desire to desegregate was not genuine though in most cases headmasters did not interpret desegregation as full co-education. Many of these headmasters had themselves been at single-sex boarding schools and wished to dilute the all-male ethos they had experienced and from which perhaps they had suffered. The decision to limit desegregation to the sixth form was a pragmatic one. It was a very much easier operation to organize and to win support for among the boys, the staff and the parents.

Another possible motive should not be ignored. Headmasters, like anyone else in a position of command, hope to leave their mark. In the wake of Marlborough's example, the introduction of girls became not only possible but fashionable; it was a significant reform for which the headmaster would take the credit in the school's history, and as reforms go, it was painless.

It will be seen that these motives did not include the wish to provide better sixth-form education for girls. As headmistresses were not slow to point out, the admission of girls seemed to have been designed primarily for the benefit of the boys. It was fair comment. Though headmasters would now argue that transfer to a boys' sixth form benefits the girls, that was not one of the arguments put forward at the time. But whatever the headmasters' motives, the girls' motives for jumping at the opportunity were essentially a desire for what they believed to be a better and richer sixth-form education.

To underand why so many girls wanted to transfer to a boys' sixth form, we need to look more closely at the girls' public schools in the late sixties. They, too, were affected by the unrest of the times, but with one or two exceptions, where girls' schools had gone to almost ludicrous lengths to ape the traditional boys' public school, they were less hidebound and possessed fewer anachronistic features that could be the subject of protest. Girls were allowed to wear their own clothes in the sixth form and to live in a sixth-form house where some of the more irritating restrictions could be relaxed.

But the girls' schools had special problems. In many cases girls entered at the age of eleven or even earlier so that by the time they reached the sixth form their restlessness owed something to the sheer boredom of familiarity. Long before the boys' schools opened their sixth forms, girls were leaving their boarding schools at the age of sixteen to go to girls' independent day schools or to maintained Sixth Form Colleges. The mixed sixth forms in boys' schools increased the flow of post-O-level leavers, it did not start it.

The girls and their parents gave other, more constructive, reasons than just a desire for change. There were four in particular; the boys' schools had a stronger academic tradition in the sixth form and higher expectations of their pupils; they took more trouble over the business of 'pastoral care'; they had a richer extra-curricular life; and finally, the mixed sixth form was a better preparation for university.

The academic argument is, like so many arguments in education, very difficult to prove or disprove. There were girls' schools whose academic tradition and performance was as strong as the best boys' schools and much stronger than the majority. Schools such as the North London Collegiate and the Perse School for Girls in Cambridge had large and successful sixth forms. There was no doubt that from an academic point of view many boys would have benefited from a transfer to such schools. But the majority of girls' schools, particularly the girls' boarding schools, were, as the Public Schools Commission put it, 'less distinguished academically and do not retain a high proportion of their pupils for sixth-form work'. Small sixth forms meant that the schools could not attract good sixth-form teachers, which in turn meant that able girls were inclined to look elsewhere for their A-level courses. Even the well-known girls' boarding schools had difficulty in attracting well-qualified staff; they did not have the resources to pay salaries comparable to those paid in the boys' schools or to provide accommodation for married staff.

Once the boys' schools started to admit girls to their sixth forms it was clear that the girls' boarding schools would find it hard to hold on to their own more able girls. What had not been anticipated by headmasters or headmistresses was that the good academic day schools would lose girls too. When Westminster decided to admit girls in the early seventies it expected that most of the applicants would come from the smaller boarding schools, but in the event three-quarters of the applicants came from London day schools with a good academic reputation.

The argument that the girls' schools had less effective systems of pastoral care is even more difficult to verify. It is true that in the girls' schools the house system was not as strong as in the boys' schools and that even the best girls' schools found it difficult to appoint good housemistresses; whereas in a boys' school a housemastership was seen as a promotion, carrying with it considerable prestige within the community, in the girls' school it was not uncommon for the housemistress to be a housemother (not unlike the dame who looked after the boarding houses in eighteenth-century Eton or Westminster), with no academic qualification or teaching role in the school. Headmistresses strongly rejected the claim that their pastoral care was less sensitive or effective, but parents and girls continued to believe that this was the case.

Headmistresses also rejected the argument that their schools' extra-curricular activities were inferior in quality or range. They could point to the high standard in music and the visual arts, by comparison with which some boys' schools were in a state of semi-barbarism. But once again the number of dedicated staff prepared and able to give time out of school was significantly smaller than in the boys' schools; and the latter were anyway emerging from their former philistinism so that the arrival of girls both coincided with and encouraged a new interest in music, art and drama.

As for the claim that a mixed sixth form was a better preparation for university, headmistresses not unreasonably asked what evidence there was. It would always be possible to find a girl who emphasized the difficulty of social adjustment from a single-sex school. In the April 1979 issue of *Learn* a former pupil of Cheltenham Ladies' College put it this way: 'You didn't then mix with young men your own age and we took a long time growing up. When you left you either went wild or sat alone in a flat reading novels and wishing somebody would come and take you out to the films.' But all this meant was that girls could be as gauche as boys in their relations with the opposite sex if they had been educated at a single-sex boarding school. If a girls' boarding school was a poor preparation for university, so was a boys'.

The headmistresses not only found the arguments for academic co-education unconvincing but they put forward counter-arguments. Schools that would remain overwhelmingly male institutions were just not qualified to help girls through the A-level years. Were housemasters with no experience of sixteen-year-old girls really capable of better pastoral care than housemistresses? The girls' minority position, where they were outnumbered in their own age group by five or six to one, would give them a distorted idea of relationships with boys which would not prepare them for the university situation, let alone for adult society. And girls of this age needed to see members of their own sex filling responsible and prestigious roles within the community and this was most unlikely to be the case in the traditional boys' public school.

Headmasters were no more convinced by these arguments than were the headmistresses by the case for the mixed sixth form. The headmistresses' arguments merited more serious consideration than the headmasters gave them. The trouble was that the headmasters did not want to discuss these issues and were inclined to dismiss the headmistresses' arguments as special pleading. Ill-feeling between headmasters and headmistresses was sufficiently strong to discourage thorough discussion of the reasons why girls were leaving their schools and of the problems they would face in the boys' schools. Some attempts were made to get headmasters and headmistresses together, notably by Michael McCrum when he was chairman of HMC in 1974, but they were not followed up. As the seventies wore on, relations between headmasters and headmistresses on this subject remained cool.

Whatever the heads may have thought, the girls voted with their feet. It will be many years before we can say for certain what all the effects of the mixed sixth form have been but we can draw some provisional conclusions.

The girls found that they had to be resilient and tough. Though the boys may have expressed themselves in favour of the admission of girls, that did not mean that they went out of their way to welcome the girls when they arrived. Girls discovered—if they did not know already—that boys could be cruel in their comments and loutish in their behaviour. Girls with brothers no doubt started without any illusions about male chivalry. Girls also found that it was essential to work out a social *modus operandi* if they were to be neither overwhelmed nor ignored. On the whole they seem to have found the boys easy to handle. Whereas the girls were sixteen when they arrived, the fast-stream boys took O-levels at fifteen or even younger, so that there could be a year's difference in age. The difference in emotional maturity—that is the ability to read an emotional situation correctly—was even more striking. Some boys wanted the girls to be mother figures, a shoulder to cry on; and girls had to come to terms with immature boys who wanted attention and sympathy but had little to offer in return. Perhaps this was the reason why intense relationships were rare. In boarding schools with mixed sixth forms, boys and girls have been expelled for being found in bed together but the number of cases seems to have been small; a fact that probably owes as much to the good sense and maturity of the girls as to the vigilance of the authorities. But most relationships between boys and girls were neither intense nor distorted by the boys' immaturity. My eldest daughter, Siobhan, who spent two years at Westminster, thought that the greatest advantage of a mixed sixth form was that a girl could have friends who were boys whereas in a single-sex girls' school any member of the opposite sex was assumed to be a boy-friend. Though some headmistresses believed that girls were moving to find boy-friends, many girls commented that they thought about boys much less in a mixed sixth form than in their girls' school.

The reactions of masters were not so easy to cope with. The girls found that the men could be more disorientated by co-education than the boys. Masters who could silence a class of boys by a facial gesture seemed quite incapable of telling a girl to stop talking or of reprimanding her if she arrived late. This in turn caused resentment among the boys. On the other hand, the girls did not find that the pastoral care of housemasters was as inept or insensitive as the headmistresses had forecast. Boys' schools that appointed mistresses or masters' wives to act in a pastoral role with the girls discovered to their surprise that the girls preferred to take their problems to men and even resented the female intrusion. Another fear of headmistresses also proved unfounded: in most schools the girls were offered and accepted positions of responsibility as house and school prefects.

As a novelty and a minority, the girls found that much was expected of them. Academically they had to aim high, if only to justify their selection. The boys' schools' expectations could also transform the girl's confidence in herself. It was true of some, though by no means all, girls' schools that they seemed ready to accept society's modest expectations of girls in career terms. One girl who transferred to a boys' school had been advised by her careers mistress to think in terms of nursing or physiotherapy; at the boys' school she was encouraged to think in terms of medicine and is now training to be a doctor. But it was not only academically that the girls aimed high. They threw themselves into the out-of-school activities more enthusiastically than many of the boys, perhaps because they had indeed been denied the opportunity in the past. They produced plays and concerts and organized community service projects. Unlike some of the boys, they were seldom blasé or apathetic. It was a bonus the headmasters had not expected. On the other hand, headmasters were disconcerted to see that the most constructive and co-operative girls could be attracted to the most roguish fringe figures among the boys. Headmasters tend to claim that the arrival of girls improved the boys' behaviour and appearance and it was probably true that in some cases a girl was more successful than a housemaster in keeping an adolescent boy on the rails.

A girl's view of the whole experience was given in the September 1979 issue of *The Elizabethan*:

The pressure to be a social success in the first few terms is very great. The boys accepted you (thought they didn't necessarily like you) if an effort was made to talk to them. They would reject you (call you arrogant, condescending) if you didn't make an effort to communicate. Once the social manner was mastered, communication had to be spread thin to maintain the number of friends you had made.

The school's sports facilities are not designed for girls (except for modern dancing class) and consequently they are allowed to do social work on one games afternoon. Intellectually the girls are set apart. Being more select, it is assumed they are more intelligent. Being female in a male society, they have to work harder than the boys to gain intellectual respect, and as it is assumed the girls work harder, they receive less respect for what they achieve. The teachers (all but three are male) also treat the girls as a different type of pupil. It is not easy to resist exploiting your feminine advantage with a male teacher and it is sometimes positively encouraged. I do not mean that a bare thigh will get you off your prep, but as most teachers are used to male societies, they are almost confused by a female pupil.

The boys of the same age, in the same class, are well-known friends with whom differences are quickly seen to be superficial. The masters and the boys in the lower school, however, continue to glance sideways. The lower-school boys' teasing is the most ruthless, and only they have the distance and time to invent cruel nicknames. I believe that if you cannot understand why and in what way you are being treated by such an amorphous mass of school boys and masters, it is easy to become excessively paranoid or at least highly self-conscious. There are ways of defending yourself and with time the situation adjusts itself. Social pressures wear off, as new girls arrive, better friendships are formed and the school becomes less alien.

The impact of the girls on the boys' society depended on a variety of factors: the number of girls in relation to the size of the sixth form, the ethos of the school when they arrived and not least the characters of the girls themselves.

It is possible, as John Dancy suggested that it might be, to detect some differences in the ethos of the schools that have for some years admitted girls to the sixth form and those boys' schools, particularly boarding schools, that have remained single sex.

The differences are those we would expect. Schools with mixed sixth forms are less likely to have retained corporal punishment; their atmosphere is more relaxed, their hierarchy less obtrusive. The girls helped to consolidate the more informal attitude of masters to pupils; masters found it almost impossible to call girls by their surnames so that Christian names became the norm for boys and girls in the upper school, both in and out of class. The girls also helped to raise the academic standard. They were not only more highly selected than the boys but usually well motivated to achieve academic success. In some schools they also helped to dilute the prevailing athleticism with a strong dose of intellectual and cultural activity. But fears expressed by the games-playing fraternity, particularly among old boys, that the school's sporting record would suffer were not borne out. Bryanston enjoyed its best ever rugby seasons in the years after introducing girls and the example of schools such as Millfield showed clearly that co-education and athletic excellence were not incompatible.

These provisional conclusions on what is still a recent innovation suggest that both the girls as individuals and the boys' schools have benefited from the introduction of mixed sixth forms. Doubts remain, however, about the wisdom of placing a comparatively small number of girls in a boys' school. Some critics argue that the boys' schools continue to treat girls as 'boys in skirts' and that the headmasters are too complacent about the success of the mixed sixth form.

The belief that co-education only works, indeed can only exist in the proper sense, when the numbers of boys and girls are roughly equal, is strongly held. It is this conviction that persuaded some boys' schools to reject the option of cosmetic co-education and to introduce co-education in the proper sense, by which they meant that there would be girls at all ages throughout the school and that not less than between 20 and 30 per cent of all the places would go to girls.

When the headmasters who were committed to co-education at all ages met in Cambridge in 1976, they gave three reasons for their commitment:

1. answering an existing social need and, based on evidence produced by several headmasters, an increasing need and demand;
2. extending the ideal of the family into education;
3. answering a growing need for places from co-educational preparatory schools.

These headmasters also re-affirmed their apprehension about the cosmetic co-education practised by their colleagues. They were convinced that they alone were the true innovators and there was a note of holier-than-thou in their criticism of the mixed sixth forms. They set up their own co-educational group within HMC and they enjoyed the support of the headmistresses. Not that the headmistresses believed in co-education but they hoped that by insisting that it should be done properly or not at all, they might slow down the fashionable trend towards the mixed sixth form. The co-educational public schools also had the support of those preparatory schools that had gone co-educational themselves. In 1979, there were 4,250 girls in boys' preparatory schools and some of the schools involved—notably Windlesham House in Sussex—had succeeded in making co-education work well in a boarding situation.

The public schools that decided to go fully co-educational went about it in a variety of ways. Some, like Bryanston, started with girls in the sixth form and then decided to admit girls throughout the school. Taunton School bought the buildings, pupils and goodwill of a nearby girls' school, thus achieving co-education by merger. In Edinburgh, the George Watson boys' and girls' schools joined to form the largest independent school in the country. In the case of Oakham, co-education was just one aspect of the school's remarkable development in the seventies under the headmastership of John Buchanan. Oakham originally took girls in the sixth form as a partial compensation for the loss of the direct grant. But Buchanan found that he could not stop there:

> So the girls arrived. It was at this point that the scales fell from my eyes and I realized that co-education was the logical conclusion to the whole civilizing process which had been gathering momentum at Oakham over the preceding decade. A monosex school, because it is operating counter to life, is basically an unnatural institution, whilst a co-educational school inevitably takes on something of a family. A delightful aspect of present-day Oakham is that nearly 400 of the 950 are siblings, and that two dozen of the faculty are parents with forty of their sons and daughters in the school. . . . So when, as inevitably happens, I am asked to justify co-education I retort that it is easier to analyse the monosex pitfalls that co-education avoids than to assess the intangible, subtle social benefits which it confers on any school. The hobbledehoy masculinity of a boys' school, which is so often accompanied by an undue emphasis on competitive games and an absence of social compassion, is at once muted in a co-educational school, whilst the limited spinsterial vision of a girls' school is at once enlarged and the stressful emotional atmosphere defused. But essentially a school should be co-educational because education should prepare for life. It is as simple and natural as that, and I applaud Shirley Williams' remark: 'The special role of women is to cease to be special.' The simple lesson which a monosex school learns on becoming co-educational is the rediscovery of a relaxed normality; one is no longer struggling to operate an inherently abnormal community.

The admission of girls to boys' public schools, whether at all ages or only in the sixth form, was in its way revolutionary. A long-established tradition was being overturned. The revolutionary nature of what happened was not diminished by the fact that progressive independent schools such as Bedales had been co-educational from the start. It was one thing to set up a co-educational school but another to admit girls to schools that had been, in some cases for hundreds of years, bastions of sexual apartheid.

There is no sign or likelihood of the revolution being reversed. The number of girls in boys' independent schools is increasing every year. Nor does there seem to be any easy way for the girls' schools to counter the attraction of the boys' sixth form. Though headmistresses have tended to reassure themselves that it is just a fashion, the underlying causes of the girls' exodus remain. Girls' schools continue to recruit at a younger age than most boys' public schools so that by sixteen some girls are restless and anxious to leave; the difficulty of appointing good teachers, particularly in science and mathematics, seems likely to increase; and the spread of co-education in Oxford and Cambridge will continue to put pressure on the single-sex sixth form in academic schools. Headmistresses will do all in their power to improve their schools and to point out to their girls the disadvantages of transferring to a boys' school, but it is unlikely that they will succeed in staunching the flow.

Relations with the outside world
There was a sense in which the old-style public school made a virtue of isolation. The world contaminated, therefore the world had to be kept at arm's length. There were exceptions of course: the city schools and day schools could not isolate themselves, though some made attempts to do so as we have seen in Harrow's elaborate defences against London and its encroaching suburbs. Isolationism made contacts with the local community rare and awkward. If the boarding school ran a boys' club, as many did, the club was situated in London, not on the school's doorstep. Charity began at a safe distance. Contact with the local maintained schools was often limited to an annual sports fixture for which the public school fielded an 'A' team, because it would never do for their first team to be defeated by a state school.

Other relationships were affected by isolationism. Parents were welcome at social functions such as speech day but were generally not encouraged to interfere in the education of their children; direct contact between parents and staff, other than housemasters, was rare. Parents accepted the schools' way of doing things, however reluctantly. The rest of society interpreted the schools' isolation as snobbishness; the schools seemed to operate like exclusive clubs, membership of which was reserved for the 'right' people. It was not enough to be able to pay the fees. At many of the more famous schools it was necessary for prospective parents to produce the names of two referees who could testify to the parents' acceptability. A parent or guardian wishing to secure a place for a boy at Harrow had to produce what were officially called 'Harrow references and connections'. Among the necessary connections at most schools was membership of the Anglican Church. Roman Catholics, Christian Scientists and Non-Conformists were tolerated but not exactly welcomed; Jews were admitted on a quota basis. The exceptions proved the rule. University College School was founded in 1830 to educate the religious minorities that were unwelcome at the established schools.

This desire to be separate, to preserve the right 'tone' and to protect the school from outside influences was increasingly in conflict with the reality of post-war Britain. In the sixties, public school boys and girls for the first time identified with a culture that had its roots in their own generation and not in their own social class. Even if a school had wanted to protect them from the influence of the pop culture, it would not have been able to do so; the transistor radio and the record player could be restricted to privileged groups but could hardly be outlawed altogether.

The sixties prised open the closed world in other ways. It was the time when greater parental influence in education was advocated, particularly by middle-class parents. Public school parents were no longer prepared to be treated as necessary nuisances. The parents' open day, a normal part of life in the day schools, came as rather a shock to the boarding establishments. Mothers went into the dormitories and often did not like what they saw. They were much less inclined than their husbands to take for granted bleak living conditions. Many fathers had been to public school themselves and may have looked upon the discomfort and the bullying as part of the training, even as part of the pleasure, just as men who survived the First World War took a certain pride in the awful conditions they had to endure. Women had seldom indulged in sentimental nostalgia for school days, but in the past they had felt obliged to go along with their husband's illusions. Now they did not. If a master failed to teach the syllabus they did not regard it as charming eccentricity but as incompetence and said so. But many fathers became more critical too. Society had moved on and they expected schools to adjust. By the mid-seventies the independent schools had had to become as open and sensitive to parental opinion as maintained schools, perhaps, as fees escalated, even more so. The paying customer relationship, so carefully played down on both sides in the past, was much nearer the surface in discussions between parents and schools, so that parental influence was an important factor in modernizing schools' attitudes and facilities.

Relations with the local community blossomed at the same time. This was partly in response to the need for better public relations; in the seventies ISIS advised headmasters to be on good terms with their locality, particularly with the editor of the local newspaper. But it also reflected a new willingness to be involved in local affairs, whether through more regular contacts with maintained schools, or as part of a developing concept of community service.

An inquiry conducted by the Community Service sub-committee of HMC in 1978, found that only three HMC schools were not actively involved in some form of community service. The majority timetabled community service against games or the CCF. The community work done by the boys and girls was impressive in its range. It was not just a question of visiting old ladies; there was work with primary schools and with mentally and physically handicapped children. This work replaced the more distant contacts with the old-style boys' clubs in the slums. The approach was different too: less self-conscious, more down to earth; it is difficult to feel like Lady Bountiful when a mentally handicapped child demands not just attention but robust physical contact.

The critics carped nevertheless, just as the headmasters tended to make exaggerated claims for the value of such work. The critics said the patronizing approach was still evident; the headmasters argued that community service opened their pupils' eyes to injustice and disadvantage in society. But both critics and headmasters missed the point. Handicapped children taken on holiday by public school boys do not inquire about motives or effects; they are grateful for the holiday. The community work had value in itself; to dismiss it as patronizing or to claim that it developed a social conscience was to give the activity an irrelevant adult gloss.

Relations with local maintained schools remained rather tentative. There were exceptions, such as Dauntsey's School which provided sixth-form education for all the local maintained schools. But that sort of co-operation was rare. As the maintained sector was gradually reorganized on comprehensive lines, relations with the independent sector became more difficult. The new comprehensive schools were struggling to establish themselves and did not altogether welcome overtures from the well-established independent schools nearby. The element of comparison and competition was inescapable. Attempts by independent schools to arrange joint activities, even offers to make their facilities available, met with some resistance from the staff of the maintained schools. For their part, the independent schools were not always sensitive to the problems of their neighbours who were suspicious of motives and had enough problems of their own without adding the uncertain blessings of links with an independent school.

Enemies of the independent schools, particularly the Labour Party, were not persuaded that the schools' new openness made them any less socially divisive. It was probably true that after the ending of the direct grant and the sharply rising fees of the seventies, the schools were even more exclusive than before. But it is important to distinguish between social divisiveness and that sense of social superiority that we call snobbery. The independent schools were bound both to reflect and reinforce social divisions so long as entry for the majority of children depended on the parents' ability to pay. But the snobbery associated with the schools in the past was much less evident during the egalitarian mood of the late sixties. The economic pressures on the middle class in the seventies changed the picture again but it was not snobbery that reappeared; the sixties' ideal of the classless society was replaced not by class consciousness but by class antagonism. By the end of the seventies independent-school pupils were likely to reflect their parents' hostility towards the trade unions and the Labour Party. The boys and girls knew their way of life was under attack and they responded accordingly; in 1969 a visiting speaker who advocated the abolition of the public schools would have won widespread support from a public school audience; in 1979 he would have been lucky not to be shouted down.

The social and economic pressures of this period also modified the independent schools' religious exclusiveness. The boys' public schools in particular had been accused of anti-semitism. Many of these schools operated Jewish quotas though they were reluctant to acknowledge the fact. In one of the most famous boarding schools of 500 pupils the quota was defined as follows:

A special class is provided on Sunday mornings and evenings for boys of the Jewish faith, of whom there may not be more than twenty-five in the School at any one time. Housemasters must be prepared, as a condition of their tenure, to take such a boy from time to time and in entering such boys for their Houses should keep in touch with the Headmaster to ensure that the quota is not exceeded.

Such definitions were not for publication.

The *Jewish Chronicle* conducted two inquiries into the question of quotas, one in 1961 and the second in 1976. The 1961 inquiry claimed to have established that in many public schools there was a 'Jewish quota' of about 10 per cent. The headmasters justified the quota on the grounds that in a Christian school it was not possible to take a larger proportion of non-Christian boys without altering the school's character and being untrue to its foundation. Fifteen years later, the *Jewish Chronicle* found that the concept of the Jewish quota had virtually disappeared and the number of Jewish children in public schools had increased, though it was said that they still experienced more difficulty than Christian boys in obtaining a place. In a number of schools the old Jewish quota had been replaced by a 'non-Christian quota'; the governors of one London school now insisted that non-Christians should not exceed one-seventh of the school's population.

A number of factors helped to modify the public schools' attitude to Jewish applicants. One was that society as a whole was more conscious of the dangers of racial and religious discrimination. Another was that after the upheaval of the late sixties the public schools took their Christian foundations less literally, or, some would say, less seriously; when a significant proportion of the boys came from homes that were not even nominally Christian it became less easy to defend the notion of non-Christian boys changing the character of the school. Finally the Jewish applicants benefited from the influx of non-Christian boys and girls in the seventies. By 1979 there were 14,000 foreign nationals in Britain's independent schools, the majority of whom came from non-Christian societies in the Near and Far East and Africa. The schools admitted them because there was a shortfall of indigenous applicants. The schools' Christian foundations that had proved such a bar to the admission of Jews turned out to present no difficulty when it came to filling empty places with Moslems and members of other non-Christian faiths.

Changes in Preparatory Schools

Although the boys and girls in preparatory schools were not as much affected by the youthful unrest of the late sixties, their schools nevertheless responded to the mood of the period. Without direct prompting from disaffected boys, preparatory school headmasters presided over changes in relationships similar to those that were occurring in public schools. More informality, more choice and more openness were once again the central themes.

Alan Mould was appointed headmaster of St. John's College School in Cambridge in 1971. He found the absence of Christian names symptomatic of the formal relationships:

In 1971 no boy here had a Christian name. He was either Smith or Smith I—but never John Smith. In fact it required some research on the part of the staff to discover what any boy's Christian name actually was. This made it difficult for them when discussing boys with parents but since this didn't happen all that often the difficulty arose only infrequently. However, what really determined me that our boys must have Christian names was standing in the Boot Room one day and hearing Ian Farbon say to his brother Paul Farbon 'Hurry up, Farbon, we're late.' Now all boys have Christian names, staff know them and they almost universally use them.

The more informal relationships once again created an atmosphere in which the use of corporal punishment declined or disappeared altogether. And just as the loosening of the hierarchy in the public schools had coincided with a decline in bullying so in the preparatory schools the relaxing of rules that had an almost monastic flavour appeared to open the way to a more civilized and gentle relationship between the boys. The headmaster of St. John's-on-the-Hill, Chepstow, commented on the effect of relaxing a silence rule of almost Trappist intensity:

When I first started teaching in a preparatory school boys did not officially talk until out in the playing field in the afternoon—getting up, breakfast, the 'bog queue', prayers, lessons, movement in the corridors, P.E. in break, lunchtime, rest and changing being all done in silence. I suppose the boys were happy in the main, but the relaxation of this discipline has brought many benefits; not least is the way in which boys now treat each other and I find that the pastoral care of older boys at all ages for their younger brethren is now quite remarkable.

Preparatory schools were more responsive than the public schools to the new style of parents. They had to be. Small in size, they could not survive long unless they were quick to respond to the changing expectations of the customers. The change from privately owned schools to charitable trusts also made it less likely that a headmaster would risk ignoring parental views. It was the preparatory rather than the public school that set up a Parents'

Association and ensured that there was strong parental representation on the governing body. Parental pressure combined with economic necessity and personal conviction to persuade some headmasters to admit girls. The number of girls in IAPS schools rose from 1,400 in 1971 to 5,000—or 6·5 per cent of the total—in 1978. As had been the case in the public schools, the arrival of girls helped to accelerate and consolidate the social changes that were already taking place. Parental wishes were also an important factor in breaking down the tradition of total boarding. Weekly boarding and Exeats made the idea of boarding more acceptable to a generation of middle-class parents, particularly of mothers, who were far from convinced that it was right to send their children away to school at the age of seven or eight.

In one respect, however, preparatory school headmasters did not follow the trend. Whereas some public schools either abolished academic prizes altogether or presented them at private rather than public ceremonies, the preparatory schools retained their enthusiasm for this aspect of competition. Young boys and their parents took an uninhibited pleasure in such occasions as the annual prize day and were quite unmoved by the arguments of progressive educationalists.

Preparatory school headmasters shared the view of their public school colleagues that the net result of the changes they did make was to produce a happier and more constructive atmosphere. They also argued that their small schools were a more sensitive weather-vane of parental opinion as expressed in the demand for places; and that the survival of so many small independent preparatory schools reflected the good sense and popular appeal of the changes that had been made.

By 1979 the impetus for change, which had its origins in the social upheaval of the sixties, was slowing down. Though independent schools did not stand still, they were no longer under pressure to relax their rules and modernize their lifestyle. The pupils, like the students in the universities, were said to be 'easier'. Boys went to chapel without protest, if not with much enthusiasm. They broke the school rules because they felt like doing so and not because they wanted to demonstrate how 'fascist' the rules were. A visit to the pub or a smoke behind the pavilion had no political overtones. There were still those who disliked the system but they kept it more to themselves. The disaffected were isolated: ignored for the most part by their peers and patronized jokingly by the masters, they could win little support. Most boys and girls wanted to get on with their lives and with obtaining the qualifications for a secure job. The young still had their own culture but the boys and girls in public schools did not identify so closely with it. The 'punks' were a working-class phenomenon, not a classless one; middle-class children could go through the motions of being part of the movement but it was difficult for them to get involved. The punks, anarchic and violent, underlined how gentle the youth movement of the sixties had been, with its emphasis on pacifism and the power of love. Headmasters may have reflected on how fortunate it was that the tough culture of the late seventies was less accessible to their boys.

The drug culture was less in evidence too; the hard line taken by many headmasters had driven the problem out of sight if not out of mind. On this, as on other matters of school discipline, it was no time for boys to be taking risks when A-level grades and the headmaster's testimonial could decide their future. As John Thorn, the headmaster of Winchester, wrote in 1978, the pendulum had not swung back; society and the schools had moved on to a new state in which economic insecurity was the common denominator:

The hyper-inflation of 1974–5, which was accompanied by no rise in tax thresholds, made greater the sacrifices parents had to make to send their children to boarding schools at all. And the rise in unemployment which accompanied the subsequent lowering of the inflation rate has made adolescent dropping-out a rare and not much admired luxury. Now, in 1978, more Wykehamists than in 1970 are thinking of how best to achieve a reasonable income level when they are twenty-five and fewer are moved by the Great Causes—the Third World, Conservation, Pacifism. Their aims now are more familiar, and more comfortable. They are the bourgeois values of 'getting on' which over a hundred years ago John Stuart Mill feared must lead to dull conformity, to the withering of originality.

Whatever the dangers of dull conformity in the 1980s, there had been lasting gains for the independent schools from the years of unrest and change. No shift of mood or emphasis in society was likely to bring back the beating of boys by boys, the personal fagging, the bullying, the often suffocating masculine ethos and the bleak living conditions dignified as 'spartan'. The independent schools had not just survived the upheaval; they had emerged with most of their more obvious blemishes and anachronisms removed. It is no accident that the public school novel, the favourite medium of embittered critics, was a vanishing genre; and that left-wing attacks concentrated not on what went on in the schools but on the wider issues of social divisiveness and privilege.

The Bloxham Project

The years of unrest and change had also prompted a constructive attempt to rediscover a Christian approach to the problems of authority and relationships in the schools. The Bloxham Project arose from a conference of headmasters and chaplains at Bloxham School in 1967. Derek Seymour's questioning of the way authority and relationships operated in a Woodard School with an explicit Christian foundation had made Bloxham the setting for this and subsequent conferences. The Project which the first conference launched had as its aim 'to inquire into the way English boarding schools communicate the Christian ideals and values to which the majority of them are historically committed'. Funded by the Dulverton Trust, the inquiry was directed by Robin Richardson and John Chapman, two young researchers who had the advantage of looking at the schools from outside, yet at the same time being sympathetic to the problems that the schools faced. The publication of the result of their inquiry in 1973 marked the end of the first phase of the Project. From that date, the emphasis was less on inquiry than on the development of the skills and insights that headmasters, house-masters and chaplains would need if they were to communicate Christian values in their relationships and in their exercise of authority. At this stage, some 120 boys' and girls' public schools were involved in the Project, whose new director, Alec Knight, a former chaplain of Taunton School, organized consultations for heads and members of staff. These consultations provided a form of in-service training that public school masters and mistresses had not had an opportunity of experiencing in the past.

It was not easy. Alec Knight and those who worked closely with him refused to provide comforting answers for the lazy or insecure. If the public schools thought that the Bloxham Project would produce a handy rationalization of the changes that occurred, they were disappointed. Headmasters in particular were challenged to examine the way in which they exercised their authority. It was not enough to be more 'liberal' in method and more 'informal' in style. The school was an organization and had to be run efficiently. Headmasters still had the power to hire and fire staff as well as to admit and expel pupils. The hierarchy may have loosened but the reality of power remained. The Bloxham Project provided a critique of this power and reinforced the need for proper consultation between those who exercised it and those who were under authority. Alec Knight also asked uncomfort-able questions about the motives of those who now put so much emphasis on pastoral care; though such work was a valuable part of the new style of relationships, he pointed out that it could also represent a need to compensate for the emptiness and hollowness of one's own life by re-ordering the lives of others. It was this sort of approach—sharp and unsentimental—that prevented the new relationships in public schools from becoming too self-satisfied and uncritical.

The Bloxham Project also helped schools to develop a new approach to religious education and to worship. In the former the independent schools were behind many of the maintained schools which had already developed new syllabuses; the Project enabled them to catch up. But it was in their approach to worship that the schools needed most help. In the wake of unrest, headmasters and chaplains had experimented with a wide range of services, only to find that the boys soon tired of innovation. Once again, the Project refused to offer easy solutions. Worship in chapel was only one aspect of the Christian community in action. If relationships in the community were characterized by thoughtlessness and ill-will, no skill or sincerity could make sense of the community's act of worship. On the other hand if relationships were informed by mutual respect for individuals as well as by awareness of the needs of the community, then what happened in the chapel was more likely to have meaning for those who attended. It mattered less whether the service was voluntary or compulsory than that it grew out of the life of the community.

The Bloxham Project could not provide Christian conviction where no such conviction existed, but it could and did help schools to communicate Christian values in a society that was secular. There were fewer convinced Christians in the schools, but there was less hypocrisy too. Public school religion, at least in the Anglican foundations, had owed as much to habit as to faith. That did not mean that there were not sincere men and women in the schools, but that there were many others who were Christians only in the sense that they were British and middle class; it was something they had been born into, not something to which they gave serious thought. Now in the seventies the old assumptions about a Christian school were no longer valid. Even the great Roman Catholic schools run by the Benedictines at Ampleforth and Downside, had to come to terms with a society in which religious scepticism was commonplace. The result was not a jettisoning of the Christian tradition, but greater humility in the school's approach. If the old confidence had gone, so had the old complacency. Headmasters and new boys were on the same journey searching for God in what appeared to be a godless world.

The Academic Revolution

If the independent schools of the seventies were uncertain where they were going on the question of religion, they had few doubts about the priority they should give to the achievement of good academic results. As the schools became less explicitly Christian and more relaxed and informal in their lifestyle, they also became more ruthless and single-minded in their pursuit of academic success.

The starting point of this new drive for academic success was the need to compete with the grammar schools for places at the universities. In the fifties the maintained grammar schools were increasingly successful competitors for places at Oxford and Cambridge; and the colleges at these universities were less inclined to take into consideration a candidate's school or family connection or athletic prowess. To the dismay of elderly dons with rose-tinted memories of the 'good college men', academic merit became the criterion for entry. For some public schools, such as Winchester and St. Paul's, this presented no problem; they had always believed in academic excellence. But for the majority it meant a change in their priorities. The independent sector as a whole could not afford to lose its connection with the two most prestigious universities which for centuries had been regarded as a natural extension of a public school education. If Oxford and Cambridge required evidence of academic attainment, then the public schools would see to it that their candidates were suitably equipped. In a characteristically English manner, institutions that had placed exam results low on their list of priorities recognized that times had changed and adapted accordingly.

The expansion of the universities in the mid-sixties and the development of the centralized admissions system with its emphasis on A-level grades as a qualification for entry, gave further momentum to the academic revolution in the independent schools. Two new factors ensured that the momentum would not slacken in the seventies. The first was the reorganization of the maintained secondary schools on non-selective lines; in 1964 only 7 per cent of the nation's children were in comprehensive schools, yet by 1979 the figure was over 80 per cent. Though there was—and still is—controversy about whether the abolition of selection and streaming by ability caused academic standards to fall, many middle-class parents believed that this was the case and looked to the independent sector to provide the sort of good academic education that had been associated with the grammar schools in the past. Parental expectation reinforced the schools' determination to make academic success the priority. The same was true at the primary level, where unstructured teaching and lack of emphasis on the basic skills drove many parents to use the independent preparatory schools for their children.

The second factor reinforcing the pursuit of academic goals was the need to justify the independent schools' existence in the face of political attack. Before the war it would have been difficult to argue that the country could not afford to lose the independent schools because of the high academic standards they represented. But by the seventies that argument was used with conviction. To some, the independent schools were performing the same role as the monasteries in the Dark Ages, keeping true learning alive in times of barbarism. ISIS argued less fancifully, but no less effectively, that it made no sense to destroy schools with good academic standards when such standards appeared to be falling in the maintained sector.

In practice, the new academic emphasis meant that the less able were excluded from the majority of public schools. In the new competitive atmosphere it was of no consequence that you had put your son's name down at birth, if he could not reach the pass mark in the Common Entrance Examination. Families that had been sending their sons to the same school for generations had to look elsewhere. As the public schools raised the pass mark they required, the preparatory schools were forced to intensify their academic pressure.

Both public and preparatory schools were accused of caring less about the intellectual development of their pupils than about favourable exam statistics. It is true that some schools allowed exam results to distort the educational perspective: one Surrey preparatory school invented a Common Entrance tie which was solemnly awarded to boys who scored more than 60 per cent in the practice papers. But the criticism that the schools were turning themselves into examination factories did not bear scrutiny; it assumed that before exam results mattered the independent schools offered a form of pure education for its own sake that encouraged pupils to develop intellectual gifts and cultural interests. But this was true, if at all, of only a handful of schools. In the majority the new academic emphasis replaced not intellectual stimulus and cultural freedom but a barren mixture of academic mediocrity and rampant athleticism.

In almost all schools in the seventies the pursuit of good A-levels went hand in hand with a flourishing of cultural activity. In 1904, Arthur Benson, Eton housemaster and subsequently Master of Magdalene College, Cambridge, wrote: 'I declare that it makes me very sad sometimes to see these well-groomed, well-mannered, rational, manly boys all taking the same view of things, smiling politely at the eccentricity of anyone who finds matter for serious interest in books, in art or music.' Seventy years later that criticism was at long last out of date. Music and art may not have commanded the universal respect that headmasters were inclined to claim, but they were no longer eccentric activities. The diversification of out-of-school activities, with emphasis on individual achievement in any field, helped to ensure that the academic drive did not produce an educational imbalance. It was just as well. Without a variety of fields in which the individual boy or girl could excel, the new-style academic school would have produced more casualties than it did.

The principal achievement of the academic revolution was that it raised standards in the many schools whose academic record had been at best modest. The established academic schools continued to do well. The following figures show the A-level results in three of the most selective boys' public schools:

School	Number of A-levels taken	Percentage grade A	Percentage grade A or B	Percentage pass grades
X	480	26	47	88
Y	437	33	54	96
Z	421	26	54	93

These are the sort of results that one would expect of a good selective school; in fact, the results are rather better than they appear because the boys in these three schools take their A-levels twelve months younger than the 'normal' age of 18. But it is the success of the less selective schools that is more striking. Here are the comparable figures for a boys' public school whose Common Entrance pass mark would be about 10 per cent lower than that for the three highly selective schools:

Q   364   17   43   92

The less selective entry produces fewer high grades but the proportion of pass grades is impressive. It is figures such as these, which could be repeated for many other less selective independent schools, that indicate just how successful the schools have been in making academic achievement a priority. What the schools have done is to enable boys and girls to reach academic goals that twenty years ago, when schools had lower expectations of their pupils, would not have been attempted, let alone achieved.

The academic revolution also ensured that the public schools would retain their dominant position in the entry to Oxford and Cambridge. They were of course helped by the reorganization of the maintained secondary schools. Oxford and Cambridge admit candidates on performance in A-level or in the universities' own entrance examination. The new comprehensive schools seldom provided the environment in which a candidate could achieve the high A-level grades required and did not have the resources to prepare candidates for the special examination. It is not surprising therefore that in the seventies the independent schools*, though containing only 23 per cent of the nation's A-level pupils, took between 50 and 55 per cent of the places at Oxford and Cambridge. What prevented them taking more were the remaining maintained grammar schools that had managed to delay or avoid reorganization. If those grammar schools were to disappear, Oxford and Cambridge would be presented with the

* i.e. independent and direct grant schools.

embarrassing problem of a public school intake even higher than a hundred years ago.

In the competition for open scholarships and exhibitions, the independent schools have been even more successful. In 1979 they won 64 per cent of the open awards at Oxford and Cambridge. The comprehensive schools won 10 per cent. The maintained grammar schools and overseas applicants accounted for the rest. Once again, if the maintained grammar schools disappeared, the independent schools would come close to sweeping the board; and rather than let that happen, the two universities would almost certainly abolish their system of awards.

Critics of the independent schools sometimes argue that these successes are made possible by an incestuous relationship between the schools and the two ancient universities. But that view is out of date. The last of the closed scholarships for particular schools were abolished in 1980 and had for many years before that only been awarded to candidates of open-award standard. The admissions tutors at Oxford and Cambridge colleges were more anxious to find good candidates from comprehensive schools than to give preference to candidates from the independent sector. They were careful to take into account any disadvantages in a candidate's education and to look for potential as well as attainment. In some cases, groups of Oxford colleges agreed to give places to comprehensive school candidates with lower qualifications than those that would normally be required for entry. But whatever the colleges do, the suspicion remains that candidates from the independent sector— particularly boys from the leading public schools—enjoy an advantage. If there is an advantage it is a question of familiarity with the admissions system. Dulwich, Eton, Manchester Grammar School, St. Paul's, Westminster and Winchester, each win fifty or more places at Oxford and Cambridge every year and it is inevitable that these schools are better acquainted, not only with the system, but also with the people who operate it.

The academic revolution coincided with changes of emphasis in the curriculum and in the careers that pupils from independent schools chose. Classics had already surrendered its preeminent position but the boom in science, mathematics and economics in the sixties and seventies made the study of Latin and Greek in the sixth form an even more eccentric activity. In 1965 all but one of the senior Queen's Scholars at Westminster took classics at A-level; in 1979, only one did, the majority taking science and mathematics. Classics departments hung on in most schools, but found it more difficult to attract the able boys. The time British public school boys once spent writing Latin verses is now spent writing computer programs. The intellectual skills required are not very different.

The popularity of science, mathematics and economics was not, as might be supposed, a crude response to the needs of an industrial society. They were popular because the boys were interested in them. Young scholars entering their public schools in the seventies were likely to list their interests as electronics, science fiction and Tolkien. They were more numerate and less literate than their predecessors; they could construct an electronic circuit rather better than an English sentence. That was the world in which they had been brought up and the world in which they would have to live. Their interests were different, not inferior or more narrow. Their interest in English literature developed later. It was one of the snobberies and delusions of the classical education that it produced the all-round man. In practice, the new-style sixth form was more likely to produce the all-round man; boys now chose three or four A-levels, often combining the study of science or mathematics with English literature or history.

In the fifties the Industrial Fund had helped independent schools modernize their science facilities and in the following decade the schools played a leading part in the development of new approaches to teaching in both science and mathematics. In the seventies, appeals for funds enabled the schools to build engineering workshops and technical centres, thus correcting another imbalance in the education they offered. It had taken three-quarters of a century for the inspiration of Sanderson of Oundle, 'the last great reforming headmaster', to be accepted by the other public schools. Despite the engineering workshops and technical centres, the public schools, like British education as a whole, retained their bias in favour of pure rather than applied science and mathematics but the old prejudice against engineering as a career disappeared. In an analysis of 14,000 boys leaving 160 independent schools in 1976/7, the Independent Schools' Careers Organization found that engineering was the most popular career, accounting for 10–19 per cent. Half the boys from public schools going to university in 1980 would be studying engineering, science or medicine. It was all a far cry from the days when Dr Arnold said: 'Rather than have science the principal thing in my son's mind I would gladly have him think the sun went round the earth. . . . Surely the one thing needed for a Christian and an Englishman is a study of Christian and moral philosophy.'

Girls' schools found it more difficult to change the emphasis in the curriculum; good science and mathematics teachers were not attracted to teaching in girls' schools, particularly boarding schools in the country, and parental prejudice against daughters pursuing such careers as engineering, accountancy and business management remained strong. The Independent Schools' Careers Organization's latest analysis shows that secretarial work is still the most popular career for girls from independent schools. But the picture is changing: in 1980 33 per cent of university entrants from girls' public schools will be studying medicine or science.

While the academic success of the independent sector in the sixties and seventies was spearheaded by a handful of boys' public schools, there was no doubt that the new emphasis on academic goals made all independent schools more efficient and more professional. Parents demanded value for money and while they were not unconcerned with such matters as good discipline and flourishing out-of-school activities, it was the best possible academic results for their boy or girl that they were seeking.

Have the independent schools then acquired a new ideology: the achievement of academic qualifications rather than the qualities of 'a Christian and an Englishman'? That is too facile an explanation of what has happened. The schools have been motivated by a determination to survive rather than by a clear ideological goal. Their approach to the need to modernize over the last fifteen years has been pragmatic. Headmasters and headmistresses have adapted the service their schools offered to meet the expectations of pupils and parents. It may not have amounted to an educational philosophy, but it worked.

7

Problems of Economics and Recruiting

Independent education is a service industry; if a school cannot attract customers it will go out of business. The aim of those who manage the school's affairs is to provide an educational service that parents will want to buy at a cost that they can afford. Incompetent management, whether of a school's educational provision or of its finances, will put the school's future at risk, as will failure to respond effectively to the challenge of inflation.

In the early seventies, as the threat of political attack from outside and of mutiny from within appeared to be receding, independent schools had to face a new and arguably more dangerous challenge. The impact of inflation in these years caused fees to rise at a rate that had never been experienced before. The average annual fee at the major boarding schools rose as follows:

1966	£545	1977	£1,785
1973	£951	1978	£2,028
1974	£1,135	1979	£2,289
1975	£1,508	1980	£2,744
1976	£1,598		

The percentage increase, 1980 on 1966, was 404 per cent; a rate of increase almost exactly comparable to that for the fifty years from 1916 to 1966. Day schools had a lower overall increase in this period, though they had to impose the largest increase in a single year, about 60 per cent on 1974–5.

For all independent schools the critical years were between 1974 and 1976 when fees felt the full impact of inflation, particularly as it affected teachers' salaries. In the year September 1974 to September 1975, the percentage increases for the different types of independent schools were:

HMC major boarding school	HMC small boarding school	London day school	Direct grant day school
32·91	35·29	52·66	62·84

Girls' boarding school	Prep schools
44·47	35·96

The rate of inflation in that year was 26 per cent, but independent schools had also to absorb an exceptional increase in teachers' salaries recommended by the Houghton Report. In 1980 they will have to absorb a similar exceptional increase as a result of the recommendations of the Clegg Commission. Average fees in September 1980 will rise from £2,744 to about £3,500.

So rapid and large have been the increases that those who work in independent schools and parents who support them have, like the citizens of the Weimar Republic, come to accept as unremarkable what only a short while ago they regarded as unthinkable. In 1979 it was difficult for them to recall with what incredulity they would have greeted a suggestion that independent schools could charge boarding fees of £1,000 a year and still attract customers. Even so shrewd an observer as Michael McCrum argued in 1976 that if the most gloomy forecast was correct and the boarding fee reached £3,000 by 1980 'it seems unlikely that English parents would be able to afford to keep their sons at Eton (or indeed any other independent school)'. Yet in 1980, with boarding fees passing £3,000, the number of pupils in independent schools reached a record total.

The success of the independent schools in confounding even their own pessimistic predictions, prompts two questions: how were the schools able to keep their places filled and how were the customers able to pay?

Headmasters and headmistresses viewed the sharply rising fees with understandable alarm. Their anxiety was increased by the knowledge that the United Kingdom birth rate had reached a peak in 1964 and declined steadily ever since. Falling rolls became a reality in the maintained primary schools in the mid-seventies, the very time when inflation was having its most dramatic effect on independent school fees. But in practice, the fall in the birth rate did not seriously affect independent schools, because the fall was relatively smaller in social classes I and II, from which most independent-school parents were drawn.

The seventies brought recruiting problems nevertheless. As boarding fees rose, the boarding market contracted. The shortage was made more acute because most schools wanted to achieve a small expansion to spread their increased costs. The battle for a share of the market began.

Even when there are plenty of pupils to go round, the rivalries between schools are only just below the surface. HMC and the other organizations of independent schools have elaborate rules to ensure that the competition for pupils is always conducted in a gentlemanly (or ladylike) manner. Outsiders are not popular. When R. J. O. Meyer started Millfield School in the thirties, the public schools in the area at first took little notice. But as Millfield became better known, largely through its success at sport, and threatened to encroach on the traditional public school market, West Country headmasters ganged up against Meyer, refusing to give Millfield sporting fixtures and providing an effective lobby against Meyer's election to the Conference. It was one of the less creditable episodes in HMC's history.

In the seventies the underlying tensions and rivalries of the independent sector were exposed. Most day schools filled their places without difficulty; it was the boarding schools that had to resort to the sort of buccaneering methods they had once condemned. Even the well-known schools could not be sure of filling their beds, though in one sense inflation helped them: it had the effect of eroding the fee differential between famous and less famous schools; it now cost no more to send a boy to Eton than it did to Abbotsholme or Gresham's.

The boarding schools responded to the crisis in a variety of ways. Many boarding schools were forced to seek new markets overseas; Hong Kong, Malaysia and the Middle East became recruiting grounds for the independent schools. Some heads even went to these areas on recruiting drives. Others relied on ISIS which set up an agency to facilitate this transfusion of life-saving pupils. The number of pupils of foreign nationality rose steadily through the seventies, reaching a peak of 14,400 or 4·72 per cent of the schools' population in 1978, since when the strengthening home market and the Iranian revolution have caused a small decrease.

The schools did not much like having to rely on foreign pupils, particularly those from cultures that had little or nothing in common with the Christian tradition the schools were supposed to represent. But they made a virtue of necessity and were as delighted with the unexpected academic honours won by the Chinese from Hong Kong as they were nonplussed by the sexual maturity of Iranian adolescents. But whether they liked it or not, many schools could not afford to be discriminating; without the foreign pupils they would have been in serious financial difficulties.

For the boys' schools, a more attractive market lay closer at hand. Once John Dancy had opened Marlborough's sixth form to girls, other headmasters recognized the possibility of using girls to balance their books in times of economic difficulty. When parental demand encouraged schools to follow Marlborough's example, there were—coincidentally—financial arguments in favour of the mixed sixth form. In a boarding school of, say, 500 pupils, it is the last ten, even five, pupils that make the difference between a surplus and a loss on the year's trading. What better way of ensuring a healthy surplus than to admit a limited number of senior girls whose arrival would cause only a minimal increase in overheads. Whatever the educational arguments, the financial arguments for preying on the girls' schools were very strong.

The headmistresses were understandably angry. At first they tried to deal with the problem through diplomatic channels. In 1975, the President of the Girls' Schools' Association wrote to the Chairman of HMC:

I have also had a very unhappy communication with other headmistresses, who feel that as the number of boys' schools taking girls into their sixth form increases, with growing inflation and rising prices, the future of the girls' schools is being endangered. I feel that we can no longer be ladylike about this and I would appeal to you, as Chairman of the Headmasters' Conference, to help get across to the heads of the boys' schools, that by creaming the sixth formers from the girls' schools, clearly for financial and perhaps for some other secondary reasons (including the welfare of their boys) they may find that before long there are no girls' schools to supply them.

But the headmasters showed no inclination to alter a policy that was being so advantageous to them. By 1977 the number of girls in boys' schools approached 7,000. The girls were contributing—at average fees for that year—some £3 million to the boys' schools' revenue. For many headmistresses the diplomatic channels no longer seemed adequate. The ladylike mask was put aside. On 27 September 1977, the *Daily Mail* reported Miss Elizabeth Manners, headmistress of Felixstowe College, as saying: 'You could put the boys' schools' headmasters on the rack and they wouldn't admit it, but their one motive in taking the girls was money. They were feeling the draught because boys were rebelling against school rules and going to polytechnics or leaving altogether. They got the girls to fill their places. They thought they might be an inducement to make the boys stay and thus stop the rot. Some of the boys' schools use totally unscrupulous means to entice pupils. . . . Often the girls who go are totally unsuited emotionally and academically. When I see the heads of these schools, I tell them they are male chauvinist pigs.'

Colourful though Miss Manners' vocabulary may have been, it expressed the frustration felt by many headmistresses. Headmasters not only removed the best pupils from the girls' schools; they defended their action with high-sounding cant about the importance of parental choice. But neither diplomatic approaches nor public recrimination could stop the flow of girls to the boys' sixth forms, because the initiative came from the customers, not the headmasters. Headmistresses refused to accept this fact, just as they refused to recognize how limited was the education offered by some girls' schools. A Marlborough house-master writing to *The Times* put it bluntly, but what he said would have been endorsed by many girls and their parents. He urged headmistresses to recognize 'the great disservice done to generations of middle-class girl pupils by the large number of potty little girls' independent schools, many now deservedly closed, where the intellectual stimulus was minimal and the cosily repressive regime set few ambitions before the unfortunate inmates beyond *cordon bleu* cookery, secretarial work and getting married at twenty.'

By 1980, the number of girls in boys' public schools had risen to 10,000. But the numbers in the girls' public schools had risen also. In other words, the headmistresses had succeeded in filling the empty places. They, too, used the overseas market and they benefited from the increasing anxiety of parents about the local comprehensive as a place to educate their daughters. And the big schools preyed on the smaller ones. The headmistresses of London girls' day schools in particular filled up their sixth form with girls from the country boarding schools while lecturing the headmasters on the wickedness of recruiting from the same source.

Both headmasters and headmistresses sought to attract more pupils direct from the maintained primary schools at eleven. Schools with an entry age of thirteen set up junior houses or provided for an Eleven-Plus entry to their own preparatory school. The argument was that in a time of inflation, if parents could not pay school fees for their child from the age of five to eighteen, they should be encouraged to do so from eleven to eighteen. But that threatened the preparatory schools, who hit back by introducing their own Eleven-Plus entry and by arguing that if money was to be spent on private education, the early years were the critical ones.

Some preparatory schools faced serious difficulties. The num-ber of schools in IAPS fell from 497 in 1967 to 449 in 1977, but the number of actual closures was few. What was happening was that preparatory schools in difficulties merged to form larger units. It was not so much a question of shortage of pupils, as of too many preparatory schools in one area. Between 1967 and 1977 the total number of pupils in IAPS schools rose, despite inflation—from 59,000 to 72,000. Once again doubts about the effectiveness of the maintained schools at this level overcame reluctance to meet the increases in fees.

By the end of the seventies the problems of recruiting sufficient pupils had been eased, if not solved. The market was volatile. Parents shopped around much more than in the past, often registering their child for several different schools and only deciding on their first choice at the last moment. One preparatory school headmaster described the new situation in these terms: 'Entry lists are extremely volatile these days. One is full one moment, overbooked the next, underbooked the next. I now ruthlessly overbook, like hotels and airlines, if I can.'

The market may have become more difficult to predict, but schools were no longer short of pupils. The 1980 ISIS census showed a record number of 366,000 pupils in the ISIS schools.

That independent schools would sooner or later price themselves out of the market has long been the hope of their opponents as well as the fear of their friends. In 1940, T. C. Worsley, in his fiercely hostile *Barbarians and Philistines*, wrote: 'Now the public schools themslves are being killed off economically. In the ordinary course of things they would probably be finished in twenty years.' At the time his view was widely shared. The thirties had been a time of cut-throat competition between the schools, thanks to a falling birth rate and what was described as 'the impoverishment of the middle classes'. But forty years later the schools and the middle class were still there, though the composition of both had somewhat changed. By the end of the seventies, it was rare to find an Anglican clergyman who could afford the fees of an independent school. Though some schools offered bursaries for the children of clergy, as a significant group of parents the clergy disappeared. It is perhaps not unduly cynical to note that the tendency for Anglican priests to experience qualms of conscience about private education dates from the time when they could no longer afford to send their children.

But as one group of middle-class parents fell behind in the race to keep up with the fees, there was no shortage of others, from investment analysts to management consultants, who were able to take their place. There were many more, too, who described themselves on their son's registration form as 'company director'.

The clientele of the independent schools did not change as much under the impact of inflation as might have been expected. 'The impoverishment of the middle classes' was a fate that many parents with children at independent schools seem to have avoided. That did not mean that families did not have to struggle to pay fees. They planned early and made sacrifices in their lifestyle. In some cases, wealthy grandparents helped. In 1978 a firm specializing in helping parents pay school fees conducted a survey of 300 clients. They found that 83 per cent of parents cut down on other household expenditure, mainly holidays and travel. Nearly 40 per cent had to find ways of increasing the household income; in most cases this meant the wife going out to work. And 29 per cent were helped out by generous relatives, usually the children's grandparents. The average parental income of those surveyed was £12,956 a year.

It is difficult to tell from these figures how much real sacrifice was involved. Most families in Britain cannot sacrifice foreign travel because they can never afford that sort of holiday anyway. Similarly, many working-class families had already discovered that it was hard to make ends meet unless the mother brought home an additional pay packet. Some middle-class mothers were only too pleased to escape from coffee mornings and church fêtes to do a real job. Women's liberation had made it easier for them. If the belief that a woman's place was in the home had persisted into the seventies, the number of children in independent schools would have been considerably smaller. The public schools were unexpected beneficiaries of radical feminism.

Tax relief encouraged many parents to plan ahead through endowment insurance policies. In other cases they were helped to pay school fees by their employers who gave 'scholarships' to the children or low-interest loans. There was also a large number of children whose parents were not paying the full fees. In 1979, ISIS estimated that between 70,000 and 80,000 of the pupils in independent schools (or about 20 per cent) were receiving financial help towards the cost of fees. This included pupils helped by the schools' own scholarships or bursaries, those helped by the variety of trusts that held money for this purpose, those receiving help from the local education authorities and those whose parents were receiving allowances from the Ministry of Defence or the Foreign Office. The number of pupils receiving help from public funds as distinct from those given scholarships by trusts or by the schools themselves was estimated at about 55,000. The parents of all children also benefited from the schools' legal status as charities. Their charitable status entitled the schools to a 50 per cent reduction in rates on school property and to exemption from certain taxes. The schools believed that their fees would have to rise between 5 and 10 per cent if charitable status were removed.

Socialist critics argue that private education receives a large subsidy from the taxpayer. The Labour Party estimated that the public subsidy to private schools in 1977–8 was at least £121 million. That total included the boarding allowances for military and diplomatic personnel, local authority funding of pupils and the tax and rate relief allowed under the schools' charitable status. The Labour Party also claimed that there were further hidden subsidies such as the public cost of training teachers who enter the private sector.

Whether the schools can be said to receive a subsidy from the taxpayer is largely a question of interpretation. The boarding allowances, for example, could just as easily (and correctly) be described as a subsidy to the government departments concerned to facilitate recruiting. Whatever interpretation one adopts, however, the Labour Party is right in seeing this as a point at which the independent sector is vulnerable.

It may not have been apparent to parents as fees rose sharply throughout the mid-seventies that the schools were doing everything in their power to keep fee increases to a minimum. The economic challenge forced schools to become more professional, particularly in their financial administration. It was a revolution in its way, overturning traditional amateurism and reluctance to exploit the financial possibilities of the school. The key figure in this change was the school bursar. The headmaster of an independent school is the chief executive; the bursar is the financial officer. Both are responsible to the governing body though the precise relationship between the responsibilities of headmaster and bursar is not always clearly defined. To say that the headmaster is responsible for education and the bursar for finance is an over-simplification; in an independent school educational and financial decisions can seldom be separated. It would be more accurate to say that the headmaster is responsible for identifying the ends and the bursar for providing the means. It is the difference between policy and logistics. But even here the separation of powers is not clear, so that there is always the possibility of conflict between the headmaster and the bursar, a conflict that has occurred in some schools with damaging effect on their performance.

When the relationship between the headmaster, bursar and chairman of the governing body (or of its executive committee) was based on mutual respect and trust, a school had a much better chance of responding successfully to the challenges of inflation. The burden of modernizing the school's financial administration usually fell on the bursar. Some headmasters had a flair for finance; rather more imagined that they did. The headmaster's principal concern was to keep the fees as low—and competitive—as possible, but he was reluctant to make the changes in policy that would cut expenditure, such as a reduction of the number of teaching staff. The bursar was not insensitive to the need to keep fees competitive, but he had to insist on a scale of fees that would cover expenditure. The bursar tended therefore to press for realistic fees and an increase in pupil numbers, whereas the headmaster and the teaching staff were inclined to resist both.

Even if he won this argument, the bursar had to exercise strict budgetary control if the school was to achieve a modest surplus at the end of the year. There were few well-endowed schools. Eton, with its income from sources other than fees of over £1 million a year in the mid-seventies, was an exception. Most independent schools had to live off fees and could not afford to make errors in their financial estimates. The largest single item in the independent-school budget was teachers' salaries; it represented 50–60 per cent of a day school's expenditure and 30–40 per cent of expenditure of a boarding school where there were other expensive overheads. Governing bodies, and to a certain extent headmasters and bursars too, were ambivalent in their response to increases in teachers' salaries. They wanted to retain and attract good teachers, but they feared the impact of large increases on the fees.

Direct grant schools and most girls' and preparatory schools pay their teaching staff Burnham Scale salaries comparable to those paid in the maintained sector. But other independent schools have their own salary scales which usually take the form of a single scale, stretching over twenty-five or thirty years. On this single scale, a master rises automatically year by year. In the autumn of 1979 a typical salary scale at a major boarding school ran from £4,500 to £10,000. Housemasters, heads of departments and other men in senior posts of responsibility received an additional allowance. It was possible therefore for a senior man in a leading public school to earn a significantly larger salary than a man of comparable seniority in a maintained school, though this was by no means true lower down the salary scale. Most boarding schools also offered subsidized housing as well as other benefits to their teaching staff, including free or cheap education at the school for their children.

The salary of a headmaster of a leading public school in 1979 was between £12,000 and £14,000 a year. In addition, he received a house rent-free and numerous other benefits in kind. The salaries of headmistresses and of headmasters of smaller schools tended to be about 20 per cent lower, but they too received generous benefits in kind. The heads of independent schools may not be rich, but they live comfortably; there are very few jobs to which they could move without a marked drop in their standard of living.

The effect of inflation on the salaries of teaching and non-teaching staff and on other essential costs such as catering, heating and maintenance of buildings, forced schools to look for new sources of finance. The principal new source of revenue was from holiday lettings. Many schools organized letting or summer schools in such a successful and professional way that the bursar could with confidence put 'profit from lettings' as a revenue item in his annual budget and mitigate the increase in fees accordingly. Marlborough, Charterhouse and Stowe were particularly successful in this field. Some preparatory and girls' schools also moved into the letting business. Two East Anglian preparatory schools, Orwell Park and Holmwood House, acted as hosts to an annual summer programme for American children; while a girls' boarding school, Cobham Hall in Kent, lets its premises at every possible moment including half-term. Cobham Hall was a good example of how an enterprising bursar, in this case a former naval officer, could hold down fees by effecting real economies and increasing the revenue by lettings.

For new capital schools had to appeal to parents and former pupils unless they were fortunate enough to have land or other possessions to sell or received an unexpected windfall from a generous benefactor. The appeal organized by a professional fund-raising firm became a familiar aspect of the independent-school scene. Headmasters proved remarkably successful fund-raisers once they had overcome their initial distaste of actually having to ask for money. No one did more to win the heads over than Dr Michael Hooker. Hooker was managing director of one of the leading fund-raising firms and made it his job to develop a unique understanding of the independent sector and in particular of its financial problems and opportunities. In many schools, Hooker's advice and encouragement was an important factor in the overthrow of stuffy and unimaginative approaches to financial administration.

Independent school appeals raised over £60 million in the years 1964–79. The two most widely used firms give the following figures: Craigmyle & Co. Ltd (formerly Hooker, Craigmyle) raised £45·3 million for school clients between 1959 and 1979;

and Richard Maurice Ltd raised £18·8 million between 1965 and 1979. In addition, a number of schools, having engaged professional fund-raisers for their first appeal, used the expertise they had acquired to run subsequent appeals themselves.

Most of the new capital raised was spent on buildings rather than on scholarships or bursaries. By 1979, the independent sector was spending £24 million a year on new buildings and equipment. Facilities, particularly in the boys' public schools, were transformed, indeed they became so lavish that head-masters sometimes expressed unease at the material benefits the boys now took for granted.

The independent schools were remarkably successful in their response to the economic challenge of the seventies. For this headmasters have tended to receive too much credit and bursars too little. The bursars' role, unlike the headmasters', did not place them in the public eye nor were they so adept at ensuring that their contribution would be recorded for posterity. Yet without efficient bursars few headmasters would be able to steer their schools through the cross-currents of this difficult decade.

Both headmaster and bursar needed the support of the governing body, particularly of its chairman. The latter ap-peared on public occasions, such as speech day, but was not otherwise in regular contact with staff, pupils and parents. If he was a good chairman he preferred to leave the running of the school to the headmaster. But behind the scenes, his role was of the greatest importance. It was to the chairman that the headmaster turned in time of difficulty. It was the chairman who was called upon to sort out differences between the headmaster and bursar or between the headmaster and his staff. And it was the chairman who had to win over the governing body to the modernization of the school, for which headmaster and bursar were pressing.

Just what could be achieved when chairman, headmaster and bursar were working in harmony is illustrated by the case of Oakham School. When the governing body appointed John Buchanan headmaster in 1958, Oakham was an obscure direct grant school of 350 boys, with an annual turnover of £40,000.

When Buchanan left in 1977, it was a fully independent co-educational school of 950 pupils with an annual turnover of £1·5 million. A combination of good chairmanship, a generous benefactor, Buchanan's drive and the financial flair of the bursar, Trevor Case, transformed a little-known school with an insecure future into one of the most successful and financially resilient in the country. The school's response to the economic threat was aggressive and enterprising. It was not just a question of trebling numbers and building a wide range of new facilities. The school also appointed a development manager to master-mind holiday lettings and went out of its way to run a successful business.

Oakham was an outstanding example of the widespread change in attitude to financial administration and planning in independent schools. In one sense, inflation did the schools a good turn; it forced them to become more enterprising and efficient. Though such generalizations are open to obvious objections, it was probably true that independent schools were being more effectively managed at the end of the seventies than at any time in their history.

Whether effective management would have been enough if the maintained sector had provided a credible alternative is uncertain. The assumption throughout this chapter has been that parents were willing to pay the ever-increasing fees for private schools because they were dissatisfied with the education the maintained schools had to offer. Whether they were right to be dissatisfied may be open to question, but that they *were* dissatisfied is not. At a critical period in the history of the independent sector, when inflation might at last have broken the will of the middle classes to pay for education, the real or imagined weaknesses of the maintained schools helped to keep the independent schools alive.

8

After the Revolution

The Conservative Party's victory in the general election of April 1979 marked the end of the period within which what I have called the public school revolution took place. It did not mean that Britain's independent schools could relax. The new government was not hostile but inflation continued and the Labour Party in opposition was bound to lay plans for a renewed attack on private education. Nor would parents be any less demanding in the standards they expected. But the schools were full, confident and well prepared, both corporately and individually, to meet whatever challenges the future might have in store.

How far had a real revolution occurred? By concentrating on a particular period in the history of independent schools, it is possible to put too little emphasis on the evolutionary element in change. In the lives of institutions there are very seldom clean breaks with the past. What happened between 1964 and 1979 was an acceleration in the pace of change; the unique combination of political, social and economic challenge operated like factory-farming techniques, forcing the schools to reform much faster and more radically than they would have done in the nature of things. Some of these reforms were revolutionary in that they overturned existing attitudes and practice. The new unity of the independent sector, the acquisition of political and public relations expertise, the admission of girls to boys' schools, the elevation of academic and cultural excellence above athleticism and philistinism, the aggressive and professional financial management, were all to a greater or lesser degree revolutionary, propelling the schools foward into a future that might in other circumstances have been delayed for a long time. Some of the revolutionary changes had their origins in earlier advances; the unity of the independent sector, for example, was a logical extension of the unity achieved by the boys' public schools a century before. Others, such as the admission of girls to traditionally boys' schools, came out of the blue. But it was a revolution without a philosophy and without leaders; there was no Rousseau or Robespierre in this story. The schools changed because they had to and because the time was ripe.

The independent schools have not reached a state of perfection nor are they free from danger. Problems and tensions remain. The unity of the independent sector has been severely strained by the controversy over whether or not to support the Conservative Party's scheme for helping parents opt out of the maintained sector—the so-called Assisted Places Scheme.

The Scheme had its origins in the Labour Party's decision to phase out the direct grant. The headmasters of the direct grant schools believed that a promising child from a poor home should be given the opportunity of attending a selective school such as their own. They were not sorry to see the old direct grant regulations dismantled but they wanted the Conservative Party to pledge itself to the introduction of a new scheme that would retain the principle but not the disadvantages of public assistance towards the fees. They envisaged central rather than local government organizing and funding a scheme under which the parent of a boy or girl accepted by an independent school could apply for financial help to pay the fees.

The Direct Grant Joint Committee, headed by James Cobban, the former headmaster of Abingdon School, put detailed proposals for such a scheme to the Conservative Secretary of State, Mrs Thatcher, in February 1972. At this stage, Mrs Thatcher did not favour the new Scheme, preferring to try and improve the existing direct grant regulations. But Cobban plugged away and in 1976 persuaded the Conservative Party in opposition to make the Scheme part of its educational policy. There had been no consultation with anyone in the maintained sector; it was just assumed that it would be better for a bright boy or girl to be educated in an independent school. That assumption tended to confirm what many critics had long believed: the heads of independent schools and the Conservative Party, despite their protestations to the contrary, knew little and cared less about what was happening in the maintained sector.

There had been no proper consultation, either, with HMC and the other organizations representing independent schools. HMC members were aware that their direct grant colleagues were trying to win over the Conservative Party to a new scheme but typically took little interest in what was going on. It was the old problem of the failure of understanding and sympathy between the direct grant and the fully independent schools; and it allowed the Direct Grant Joint Committee to commit the independent sector to a policy, the details and implications of which were known only to a minority.

It was at this point—in 1977—that I became chairman of HMC. Like so many of my colleagues, I had not taken the trouble to think through the implications of the Assisted Places Scheme. When I did so, I was convinced that the Scheme was a mistake, that it would alienate the maintained sector and make it more difficult in the future to find ways in which the two sectors could co-operate. The Scheme was based on a false premise: that an independent school was automatically a better place to educate a bright child. But in some parts of the country, the maintained schools were perfectly capable of enabling a bright child to fulfil his potential. To help parents move a child in those circumstances would be a waste of public money and an insult to the maintained sector. The Scheme contained no safeguard against such a move being made at public expense, because it did not provide for any consultation between the heads of the maintained and independent schools. The heads of the maintained schools would just have to acquiesce in the loss of their brightest pupils; without trial or consultation their standards would be found wanting. It is not surprising that the Scheme has been unanimously condemned by those who work and believe in the maintained sector.

As chairman, I insisted that the details of the Scheme should be sent to all members to be discussed at their divisional meetings. But I was too late; once the Scheme had been adopted by the Conservative Party, the heads of independent schools shrank from expressing their doubts. At HMC's annual meeting in Oxford, I used my chairman's address to sound a note of caution nevertheless:

> The Scheme is a topic for discussion in HMC Divisions this term. I hope you will take that opportunity of considering all its implications . . . it is clearly important that any political party should know HMC's view as fully and accurately as possible. Some members of HMC, I know, think the Scheme has been taken too far, too fast. Others are anxious that we should not encourage any political party to adopt the wrong priorities at a time when there is an acute shortage of money for education.

But the warning was not heeded. Between 1978 and 1980, when I was no longer chairman, I conducted a more outspoken campaign against the Scheme in speeches and in articles for the press. It made me unpopular with my colleagues and did nothing to discourage the Conservative Party from going ahead with the Scheme when they came into office. When the Scheme begins to operate in September 1981, it will have the support, if not the active participation, of all but a very few of the heads of independent schools. ISJC is firmly committed to the Scheme. To the Scheme's supporters it represents not only a useful injection of public finance and clever children, but also an official recognition that there is a role for the independent schools as centres of academic excellence. The small minority who oppose the Scheme believe that it represents a short-sighted attempt to syphon money and talent away from the maintained sector without any check that there is a real need for such children to be moved.

The controversy over the Assisted Places Scheme strained but did not break the newly established unity of the independent sector. But the controversy did underline that there was no agreement within the independent sector on what contribution independent schools should make towards the national provision for education. In the wake of the public school revolution it is this question that remains the most important both for the schools and for their opponents. Until 1979 the schools were preoccupied with survival. The Conservative Party has since helped the schools financially with tax changes and with the Assisted Places Scheme. It has also created a climate in which independence and excellence are not regarded as anti-social. But the Party has not given much constructive thought to the problems that independent schools raise. In Britain, as in other countries such as Australia, a flourishing independent sector does exacerbate divisions in society and creates—or at least appears to create—inequality of access to opportunity. There are those who believe that the only solution to these problems in a democracy is for all the maintained schools to reach the high standards that some already achieve, so that parents will no longer wish to spend large sums on private education. I share that view because it seems to me the only one that reconciles the demands of equal opportunity and of liberty. But it is not a view that carries conviction unless those who hold it are seen to make the improvement of the maintained sector their priority. So far the Conservative Party has failed to convince its critics that this is their aim.

Labour's view of the role of independent schools is more explicit, but no more convincing. In July 1980, the Party published a discussion document on *Private Schools*. The document proposed the elimination of independent schools by the method once favoured by Roy Hattersley: making it illegal for schools to charge fees. The Secretary of State and the local authorities would be given enabling powers 'to publicly own those schools which they require for community purposes'. As a preliminary step, Labour would squeeze the schools financially by removing their charitable status and stopping all funding of pupils at independent schools by local authorities and government departments.

The document caused little stir. The schools and their opponents had heard it all before, and there was little evidence that the new Labour spokesman on education—Neil Kinnock—

would be any more successful than his predecessors in generating the political will to put abolition into practice. Labour was more likely to find the political will to squeeze the schools financially, though even here the difficulties already encountered over the question of charitable status and the opposition of the armed forces and the Foreign and Commonwealth Office to the ending of boarding allowances would not easily be overcome.

The Labour Party does face up to the problems of divisiveness and inequality posed by the independent sector, but its solutions are invariably negative and ignore the claims of liberty. Like the Conservative Party, Labour appears to be curiously reluctant to believe that the problems can be solved by an improvement of the maintained sector, preferring to argue that the maintained schools will never improve until the independent schools have disappeared.

The heads of independent schools are in the habit of saying that they want the maintained schools to improve. That is an admirable sentiment but like other admirable sentiments on the lips of headmasters, such as the proposition that 'this hurts me more than it hurts you', it is received with a degree of scepticism. I find my own attitude ambivalent. The improvement of the maintained schools is in the national interest as well as in the interest of the boys and girls concerned. While I hope that improvement will be achieved I do not expect or wish the independent sector to wither away. The advantages to society of having some schools that can go their own way and if need be defy the government or the prevailing educational orthodoxy are very great. The independent schools have refused to follow the fashionable belief in the virtues of non-selective secondary education. It is not a question of whether in doing so they are right or wrong. What matters is that they are free to choose their own policy. A different example of the advantages of independent education is provided by South Africa. In that country the state imposes ethnic divisions in education which the government schools have to accept. But the independent schools can and in some cases do defy the government and admit children of all races. The Afrikaaner-dominated Nationalist

Government shares with the British Labour Party a profound suspicion of the freedom enjoyed by independent schools. That is not as ironic as it sounds: both political groups have an almost messianic conviction in the rightness of their cause and a consequent hostility towards those who do not conform.

The absence of a constructive approach by either major political pary in Britain means that there is no prospect of a political answer to the question of what contribution the independent schools should make to national education. The Conservative Party does not believe there is a problem; the Labour Party does not believe there is a solution short of abolition. The emergence of a new centre party, free from socialist dogma and more interested than the Conservatives in equal access to opportunity, would change this situation, but for the time being the independent schools must chart their own course. While remaining open to constructive proposals for co-operation with the maintained sector, they will concentrate on the more immediate problem of continuing to provide an education that parents will want to buy at a cost they can afford. To idealists, that will appear a low, even sordid, aim. To the pupils in the independent schools and to their parents it will be the right one.

Index